KUNDALINI EXPOSED

KUNDALINI EXPOSED

Disclosing the Cosmic Mystery of Kundalini.

The Ultimate Guide to Kundalini Yoga,
Kundalini Awakening, Rising, and Reposing
on its Hidden Throne.

- BOOK 3 -

SANTATAGAMANA

Version 1.2 – Updated October 2018

Special thanks to Eric Robins, who edited and proofread this book with profound love, kindness, and dedication.

Cover art: Titima Ongkantong/Shutterstock.com

Read also, by the same author of *Kundalini Exposed*:

— KRIYA YOGA EXPOSED

The Truth About Current Kriya Yoga Gurus & Organizations. Contains the Explanation of a Special Kriya Technique Never Revealed Before.

— THE SECRET POWER OF KRIYA YOGA

Revealing the Fastest Path to Enlightenment. How Fusing Bhakti & Jnana Yoga into Kriya will Unleash the most Powerful Yoga Ever.

— THE YOGA OF CONSCIOUSNESS

25 Direct Practices to Enlightenment.
Revealing the Missing Key to Self-Realization. Beyond Kundalini, Kriya Yoga & all Spirituality into Awakening Non-Duality.

— TURIYA: THE GOD STATE

Unravel the ancient mystery of Turiya—The God State. The book that demystifies and uncovers the true state of Enlightened beings.

— SAMADHI: THE FORGOTTEN EDEN

Unveiling the ancient art of how yogis and mystics had the keys to an unlimited reservoir of wisdom and power. This book brings the timeless and forgotten wisdom of Samadhi into modern-day practicality.

— THE YOGIC DHARMA

Revealing the underlying essence of the Yamas and Niyamas.
A profound, unconventional, and inspiring exposition on the spirit of the Yogic Dharma principles.

Available @ Amazon as Kindle & Paperback.

Subscribe and receive the ebook **Uncovering the Real** plus updates and information regarding new books or articles, which will be sent about once a month.
www.RealYoga.info

If you have any doubts or questions regarding this or any of the other books, feel free to contact me at:
Santata@RealYoga.info

He who is in the Fire [Kundalini],

and he who is in the Heart [Spiritual Heart],

and he who is in the Sun [Consciousness],

they are one and the same.

- M<small>AITRAYANIYA</small> U<small>PANISHAD</small>

TABLE OF CONTENTS

INTRODUCTION

Forget all Kundalini books.

This is not a guide written by a scholar who only dwells in the realm of theory. The awakening of Kundalini requires direct experience, not an academic degree or a theoretical dissertation.

This is not a guide written by a monk who took secret vows and can't really reveal anything, but then produces a 400-page tome full of Kundalini rhetoric because the useful and real teachings are only for the "high initiates."

Most Kundalini books are either very abstract, occult, esoteric, with hidden information so as not to "enrage the Masters," or very "Goddess," "physically focused," "Westernized Yoga." Both categories will hardly help a genuine aspirant. Most of the time, the first one will be nothing more than a labyrinth of thoughts posing as "genuine knowledge," arousing intellectual satisfaction. The second one will be too superficial and not really pointed at true enlightenment.

This book is a guide written by someone who practiced Yoga in its full profundity and has successfully awakened the Kundalini all the way to its resting "place," which I'll tell you right away, breaking the first common misconception—it's not in the head. All of this is being shared without ever being compromised by a guru, an organization or a tradition. My words are free from an agenda. This book is not for followers of any tradition in particular, but for those whose heart and mind are open to receiving love and wisdom.

I will share rare Kundalini wisdom and practical instructions that actually work, not just theory from a forgotten ancient scripture or found on the "Akashic Records." We don't need more complex practices that just lead to mental noise. Only straightforward and powerful teachings are worth it.

This publication will give real and direct first-hand knowledge about Kundalini based on my direct experience, not from reading books or hearing stories.

Most books about Kundalini talk how when it is awakened it goes up through the spinal cord until it reaches the Crown Chakra, where *Samadhi* or an ecstatic experience will occur. That is indeed quite an accomplishment, yet it falls short of reaching its true goal—the Spiritual Heart.

The Spiritual Heart (not the Heart Chakra) is not well-known in spirituality. This book will explain and unveil its nature, in a clear and understandable way.

Additionally, I'll disclose the different levels of Kundalini awakening, its journey, and its relation to Consciousness and Being. You will know why awakening this primal energy is of utter importance.

I'll also give helpful tips on how to prevent "Kundalini syndrome," for a safe awakening of the Kundalini energy. Living with an awakened Kundalini doesn't have to be a burden. It's a divine gift, one that we'll use to reach the depths of the spiritual path, leading us all the way to enlightenment.

No Kundalini questions shall remain unanswered. If they do, you will know how to go one step further and dissolve the questioner, so that the eternally-questioning-ever-doubtful-ego is no more.

The Truth will then shine through you, in its purity. Kundalini Shakti will finally merge with Consciousness Shiva, forever reposing in the Heart Throne!

Your spiritual enlightenment purpose will finally be fulfilled.

Part 1

CHAPTER 1

THE GOAL

Happiness. Isn't that what we are all looking for? Every action a human being takes is in the pursuit of happiness. Happiness is our call since we are motivated to achieve what we think will make us happy. Think about what you really wanted five years ago. Do you still want the same thing now? Probably not. How many times have you achieved what you wanted and afterwards realized it was empty?

"Okay, I achieved what I wanted... now what? Something is still lacking." After the brief enjoyment you experienced when your desire was fulfilled, your reaction was probably similar to the above sentence.

Think about what you really want right now. Be honest. What are you really looking for? It doesn't matter what it is, for one thing is certain: you believe that having or achieving what you really want will end all your problems, sorrows and constant dissatisfaction.

Humans have been trying to find happiness and satisfaction by external means for eons, with no success. Do not expect to answer any questions or solve any problems with an external solution. They originate internally and so does the solution.

It is time to stop. It is time you look inside and make a commitment with yourself and affirm: "I will find that which I'm looking for." You don't even need to call it happiness. Call it "What I Really Want."

You might not even know that what you want *right now* is *That* which this book points at, which despite being given many names such as enlightenment, is verily nameless.

Let the energy behind the words of this book guide you toward *What You Really Want*.

You can do it. Do you know why?

It's not something out there, something that you have to reach for. It is already in you. You just have to remove the ego-cloud that seems to cover the blissful sun of Consciousness.

Achieving *What You Really Want* will end all wants, all desires, and all pursuits. *That* by which "having it," you'll be eternally fulfilled, never wanting anything else—let's say it like that. *That* is *What You Really Want*.

This is not a mundane subject. It is about the root of suffering and the eternal longing for what humans "really want"—happiness, peace, love and fulfillment.

"But what has all that to do with Kundalini?"—You may ask.

Kundalini is the *single most important aid* you can use to help you achieve *What You Really Want*. Let's explore it!

CHAPTER 2

KUNDALINI

There are many different Kundalini definitions. A simple and straightforward one is that Kundalini is the latent cosmic energy inherent in every living being. Although it is a very misunderstood phenomenon, all forms of spirituality require a Kundalini awakening. *Samadhi, Yoga (Union), Nirvana, Mukti,* Salvation, Enlightenment, Self-Realization, whatever name we wish to give to the ultimate state of Consciousness, it always requires the awakening of Kundalini. Awakening it is synonymous with the awakening of the unconscious. You can never realize your true Being unless all the unconscious parts of your illusory identity come to the surface and you recognize them not to be you.

Although many esoteric and symbolic terms are used to describe the Kundalini, we will demystify it in the simplest of ways—it is just *prana*, the life-force, but a huge reservoir of it, the primal power.

Many people believe it is a malevolent power or something ridiculous like that, but how can your own life-force, that which sustains your life, be bad? Those assumptions are merely religious dogmas and we will stay away from them. It is also pictured as a sleeping serpent coiled in *Muladhara*, the Root Chakra, because some yogis have experienced it as a "powerful serpent aggressively going up," but there is no serpent anywhere.

Instead of using mythological representations to explain Kundalini, let's use a modern and unambiguous example:

To be able to turn the lights on, do an internet search, have the fridge working, turn on a fan, air conditioning or any other electrical device, a house needs electrical power. Without it, none of those things will work. All that power is provided through high-voltage transmission lines, yet upon reaching a house, its voltage is stepped down and greatly reduced in order to prevent burnout. There the electricity travels through wires inside the walls to the outlets and switches all over the house.

Those wires are analogous to your nervous system, which is said to be composed of thousands of subtle energetic channels called *nadis*. Prana, the life-force which runs through them, can be equated with electricity. If your body (house) only requires around 500 kWh to keep going and survive, it will never improve and adapt to a higher voltage. To run a super-computer rather than a normal laptop, your current voltage wouldn't work. Hence we need to increase our body's pranic capacity so that we can use more life-energy.

Now imagine we went all the way back to the power plant, where the original electrical generators are, and plugged directly into that whole energetic load rather than reducing it to accommodate our house's capacity. What would happen? Our entire electrical system would fry. This example is akin to awakening the Kundalini unprepared—it's way too much energy coursing through a system that hasn't been prepared to handle such high voltage.

That being said, cases like that are rare. What usually does happen is the partial awakening of Kundalini in people who are little or semi-prepared, and this is one of the reasons they can experience a wide variety of symptoms. If you are reading this book, there's a high chance you've already meditated or done some spiritual practice, even if just in a previous life-time.

Many yogis and ancient texts overcomplicate this whole process, talking how one's system needs decades or even lifetimes of preparation to awaken this primal energy. The truth is that we don't have decades or lifetimes. All we have is the now. I'm not talking about a magic pill, but about taking an entirely different and direct approach. Is it possible, then, to do it faster? Yes. I have done it, and there are many cases of people who have done it faster than the conventional "decades or lifetimes of preparation." Usually, the more you are surrounded by such preconceived ideas and dogmatic people, the longer you will take.

I have found out that there's a threshold of purification that people must go through to bypass any strong side-effects, but beyond that, any slight side-effects experienced can be managed and overcome with ease.

Let's say all meditations and spiritual practices have an energetic level of potency from zero (doesn't do anything) to ten (super powerful).

Let's also say that the system's capacity of every human being goes from zero (never did any meditation or anything related to spirituality in this lifetime or another) to ten (ripe for enlightenment).

Lastly, we will assign a grade for how unbearable the side-effects of Kundalini awakening are. Zero means no negative side-effects, and 10 suggests bedridden, or something awful.

Level of Symptoms experienced	
0 - 2	No problem
3 - 4	Acceptable
5 - 6	Tough
7 - 8	Hard
9	Very hard
10	Chaotic

The more powerful the practice is, the higher the system's capacity needs to be. For example, a practice level 10 requires a system capacity with at least level 6 to experience between 0 and 4 of symptoms level. Also, remember that just because a beginner has no previous meditation experience, this doesn't mean his or her system is level zero. No, it can be dormant and quickly adapt to a high level, 6-8, for example. It would not be the first time I've seen it. We need to take a broader vision and recognize that a person's "spiritual history" is not confined to this lifetime.

To do the math of how powerful the side-effects will be, you must subtract the System's Capacity from the Potency of the Practice, and this will give you the possible level of symptoms.

An aspirant doing a level 8 spiritual practice with a body-mind's capacity of level 4 will experience a degree of side-effects between 0 and 4 (8-4 = 4).

Another example: spiritual practice level 4, system's capacity level 4 = no side-effects. Someone whose system's capacity level is higher than the spiritual practice power will also not experience any side-effects. In cases like this, however, the spiritual evolution of such a person will be pretty slow. That's why you need to continually improve your practice until no more practice is necessary, and you've reached a "no-practice-beingness" level.

Improving your practice doesn't mean switching it up. It can be as simple as doing the same practice but with better concentration and surrender, or increasing the amount of time you're practicing, switching up the focal point to something more powerful, or adding a new component like a *mudra* or a *bandha*.

Regarding the side-effects, as long as they are below or equal to 4, it's fine.

Kriya Supreme Fire, one of the strongest Kundalini practices, starts at around level 7. But hold on! Before you turn around, don't worry. You can always begin with a super easy preliminary practice without any chance of having any negative side-effects. Anyhow, this powerful practice is the perfect combination of a fast and potent Kundalini awakener that really works, with an acceptable level of symptoms experienced. By increasing the amount of time we do this practice, we can go from level 7 up to level 9. The more you do it, the higher the potency level is.

A more accessible practice, around level 4, would be the single *Kriya Pranayama* as described in *Kriya Yoga Exposed*. A stronger practice, level 10, would be the full routine as described in *The Secret Power of Kriya Yoga*.

All of these numbers might get a bit adjusted when we add in grounding methods or other practices (like some *asanas* or mudras), which always retain the potency of the original practice, but also increase the system's capacity and thus help to lessen any negative side-effects. On the other hand, they also require more time and dedication which many people can't afford. Nevertheless, if you follow the practices and the "grounding" tips as suggested in this book, you will be looking at 0-4 for side-effects experienced. Remember that all systems are different, and your experience might deviate from what is being written here.

Coming back to the electricity metaphor, we will learn how to tap into the "power plant" reservoir and awaken it, so that we can progress faster in the evolution of consciousness from a personal consciousness toward the Universal Consciousness and beyond.

Harnessing and awakening this energy will change your life. Not only it is the essential carriage of your journey toward enlightenment, but it is also beneficial if you just want to have a better life, free from disease, and full of vitality, energy, and joy.

In the old days, every student had a Guru to guide him toward the awakening of Kundalini. Nowadays, in this modern era, that's not possible. Most people have no time or motivation, and unlike in ancient India for example, society is not built in a way that facilitates the transmission of such knowledge. We don't hear about these teachings from an earlier age, nor do we go searching for a Guru as soon as we finish our primary education.

Thanks to the internet in particular, written instructions and knowledge can flow faster from one side of the world to the other. We no longer have to go to a secret library in an underground temple to read ancient scrolls in a forgotten language. That would certainly be an exciting adventure, but one that would have a high chance of being unsuccessful.

Although the physical presence of a genuine being—one whose Kundalini is reposing in the Spiritual Heart—is extremely helpful, such pure beings are not easily found. Rarely will you encounter them in "mass commercial initiations." We must also remember that the true Masters are always available, ever-present within our own consciousness, for time and space do not limit them. We just need to open ourselves to their constant blessing.

Sincerely practicing and connecting with the Guru within, alongside reading practical and truthful instructions without too many ambiguities (such as the instructions transmitted in a book like this one), constitute a superb way to walk the path without being distracted or misled by dogmatic spiritual organizations.

In this book, it's not so much about the words you are reading but about the energy behind them and where they are pointing (the Source) that make a difference. Reading it like you would read a newspaper won't cut it. You must be engaged in the "energetic field" of the book, letting the essence from where these words come fill you up, and guide you deeper and deeper within, piercing through many layers of mind-noise toward your pure nature.

DIFFERENT LEVELS OF KUNDALINI AWAKENING

There are different levels of Kundalini awakening.

Each level corresponds to a Chakra. There are seven main Chakras:

1. Muladhara (Root Chakra)

2. Swadhisthana (Sacral Chakra)

3. Manipura (Navel or Solar Plexus Chakra, in the spine at the level of the navel)

4. Anahata (Heart Chakra)

5. Vishuddha (Throat Chakra)

6. Ajna (Brow or Third Eye Chakra)

7. Sahasrara (Crown Chakra)

You have probably heard or read a lot about the Chakras. Here, we will not go deep into the explanation about each one of them, as that would miss the purpose of this book.

Typically, the vital force flows through the subtle side channels, *Ida* and *Pingala*, which are located on either side of the spinal column. Humans spend their lives swinging between both of these channels, which symbolize duality.

When the Kundalini awakens and travels upward, it goes through the *Sushumna Nadi*, the subtle central channel in the spinal cord. As it rises, your awareness becomes very subtle and brilliant, "connecting" with the subtle body and inner senses, going through each one of the main Chakras. Whenever it reaches some Chakra, a Chakra-based experience might happen for the meditator—wonderful visions, fabulous scents, otherworldly sounds, etc. These are amazing experiences, but they do not last forever, and the bliss and awe one feels when they occur rapidly fade away, minutes, hours or days later. You might even acquire temporary supernatural abilities, but those too will pass. We should enjoy those experiences, but not get too attached to them.

If you catch a train in Tiruvannamalai, South India, with the purpose of arriving in Srinagar, in the Indian Himalayan region, you will pass by many stations. Although it might be tempting to take a side excursion by leaving from Agra station to visit the Taj Mahal, would it serve any purpose? That's like an experience with a Chakra.

Many think these experiences are Self-Realization or the final Liberation, but that's only self-deception. Rather, these seekers "fall" prey to those phenomena and never go beyond them. It might be fun for a while, but ultimately, they will not lead you to your final destination. None of these experiences are *That* which you are looking for. This is because what you are looking for is always the subject and never the object. An experience (object) implies an experiencer (subject), being always dependent on it.

Some people awaken the Kundalini involuntarily, for example, due to past life spiritual practice, a near-death experience, tremendous suicidal depression, or a combination of these, which might be a source of problems. Many people don't even know that they have an awakened Kundalini and instead might think they are crazy.

The final level of the Kundalini—the Spiritual Heart—is beyond chakras and unrelated to an awakening. It is a dissolving, which is where, ultimately, we are headed to. It is also called *Hridaya* or the *Temple of the Heart*. That's our Home.

CHAPTER 3

CONSCIOUSNESS

Throughout this *Real Yoga Series*, we've often talked about Consciousness. Yet many people are still not entirely sure what it means. Let's clear all doubts right now:

Consciousness is *That* which is conscious. Is your body conscious? No. Is your brain conscious? No. We could go on all day, until we realize that nothing is conscious by itself, except Consciousness.

It is this background of Consciousness that allows everything to be. The world and everything you perceive, from gross physical objects to subtle feelings to even subtler thoughts— all are perceived by you, by your Consciousness.

This means Consciousness is like a movie screen while all objects are part of the movie. The mind creates the movie itself. In the movie, we have suffering, wars, death, and so on, but the screen stays untouched. For this reason, Consciousness has never suffered. It is stainless, ever pure.

The ancient rishis in India called it *Brahman* or *Parabrahman*, while others, like the yogis, called it *Shiva* or *Parashiva*. In the west, they called it *God*, although this word has been adorned with a multitude of dogmas, beliefs and even a form, which is always limiting.

Since Consciousness is formless, people had a hard time connecting, understanding, and surrendering to it, so they gave it a name and were taught to worship it as an anthropomorphic being (Shiva for example). This allowed them to connect somehow to the divine, to their true essence, in a more accessible way. The idea was that this would purify their minds enough to go past the forms into the formless. All those words and anthropomorphizations are just symbolic names for the screen of Consciousness.[1] In this day and age, especially in western countries, the veneration and adoration of symbolic entities is falling abruptly mainly because of the technological and scientific standards of new generations, and the association of such "beings" with corrupt, dogmatic or sectarian religions.

---

[1]Even Kundalini and energy were anthropomorphized and given lots of different names, like Shakti. Sometimes, I use those names (Shiva and Shakti) since they convey the principles of Consciousness and Energy to aspirants who are more devotional in nature.

Returning to the screen example, we can easily understand how Consciousness stays immaculate despite what happens in the movie. Currently, the vast majority of humans identify themselves with the movie and its characters (ego-mind).

Those who want to wake up from this mass delusion have to recognize their true essence as the eternal and ever-pure screen of Consciousness, disidentifying from the temporary and restless false self known as ego.

The screen of Consciousness is always there, even in unconscious states. What is not there is this personality that we believe we are, whose source is the mind, the thought "I."

Raising the Kundalini will give us access to the depths of what we thought was unconsciousness, but is actually profound bliss. We will stop paying attention to the movie and instead turn it toward the screen that has never suffered, the substratum where every movie plays.

Although Consciousness always remains unmanifested, it has the potential to become anything. It is through the cosmic energy (Kundalini) that Consciousness manifests. With that said, Kundalini is also Consciousness, like a mighty ocean-force that creates waves in what would otherwise be a still ocean.

Kundalini Shakti (Mother, dynamic energy, manifested) will *meet* Consciousness Shiva[2] (Father, unmovable consciousness, unmanifested).

BEING

The intrinsic nature of Consciousness is "Being." Not only is Being beyond the countless forms of life that come and go, but it is their very essence. It is our true nature. We are human *beings*, not human *doings*. To be is to be conscious.

The dimension of Being is right here, right now. It doesn't have to be reached, yet our cloudy minds make it seem like an arduous and distant achievement. With a still mind, we can easily recognize it in us. At first, it might be felt as a profound experience of stillness, peace, joy, etc., but as one goes further, it will dissolve our individuality and our blissful Oneness will shine through.

For the majority of humans, the beingness-state is experienced involuntarily, perhaps a couple of times in their lifetime, always without the acknowledgment of what it really is. It is unfortunate but true that most people live and fluctuate

---

[2] Sometimes, it is also called Christ Consciousness. Some traditions view Christ Consciousness as the Absolute Consciousness, while others see it as the Universal Consciousness (unitive mind), which encompasses the whole universe but not beyond it toward the Unmanifested.

only between different levels of "zombieness," never having a conscious recognition of the true Life within them. When the mind is in a "state of being," it is peaceful and free of concepts. Past and future, which are only memories and thoughts, have been extinguished.

All this must be known through direct experience and not through intellectual knowledge. Words can only get you so far. You must dive deep within and find the pearl of Being-Consciousness.

ENLIGHTENMENT

It is time we find ourselves beyond the confines of a mundane and limited existence.

Sometimes, we have flashes of something beyond, something beyond our everyday life. If only for a brief moment in time, we "experience" our Beingness beyond this limited self.

Any form of happiness, bliss, joy, ecstasy, contentment, fulfillment, pleasure, peace, etc., is but a glimpse of the true bliss (*ananda*) of our true nature (*sat-chit-ananda*, Being-Consciousness-Bliss). All these glimpses mostly occur after a desire has been fulfilled, which makes the mind temporarily desireless and able to enjoy its natural joy.

Most humans' goals are related to being rich, powerful or having sexual relations and physical intimacy because that's where they get their little "fleeting" joy, their pleasure. The feeling of completeness and enjoyment they get from these achievements and moments causes them to drown in those superficialities even more.

"With money I can please all my desires, therefore, I will be happy. People will bend to my will for I am rich."

"With fame, the world will accept me. Having a high social status makes me happy since people respect and look up to me."

"With sex, I feel tremendous pleasure, and I am fulfilling my need for love and physical connection. I want more and more sex because in those moments I am 'out of myself,' in ecstasy (the same happens with drugs)."

The moments when people are in alternate states of consciousness that are more blissful than their normal state are during sexual union/orgasm, when they are under the influence of mind-altering drugs, when they are listening to a song they really love, during those ten seconds after their team won the Super Bowl, when they meet their idol whom they have put on a pedestal, etc.

What is also common during these experiences is that the feeling of "I" is "shrunk" or "forgotten" for a short period, allowing much joy. Obviously, this is far away from the true happiness of being that is inherent in every soul.

Just as the whole tree is potentially present within the minuscule seed, enlightenment is present within a human being. We only have to blossom beyond our personhood.

Searching outside for fragments of happiness, fulfillment, acceptance, shelter, or love will never truly satisfy you. You have a treasure within that not only holds all those elements, but is infinitely vaster than anything the universe can give you. Once you "know" the pure bliss of Being, all external happiness becomes meaningless.

This treasure has been given many times. Nowadays, many people call it "enlightenment." This subconsciously creates the idea of something far away, something impossible for the common human, something that is not present in ourselves already. This is the ego's game, trying to hide and elude us of our peaceful natural state of Beingness. This inherent state is a state of oneness with "something" unfathomable and deathless, which is what we really are in our deepest core, beyond all forms.

CHAPTER 4

The Importance of Kundalini Awakening

Kundalini awakening is the primary factor in human development, evolution (outward expansion) and involution (internalization toward unity).

As human beings, we base much of our understanding of life on our direct perceptions and knowledge, both of which are brought about by the five senses.

I perceive this table; I am conscious of your suffering; I see the sky; I hear Beethoven's *Für Elise*, and so on. At the same time, there are a majority of "things" that happen that I do not directly perceive or am not directly aware of. I might see and smell a tasty green apple, and I eat it consciously, but the digestion and assimilation process is done unconsciously. If I accidentally cut my hand with a knife, the body will heal itself, but this is done unconsciously. Usually, people are either unaware of these processes or do not take conscious control of them. Yet all those involuntary actions are done by them.

All processes can be brought up to the conscious mind. Some are easy to do, some harder. Take for example breathing—it is going on effortlessly. Humans are not breathing consciously. Yet if they want to—and this is one of the most natural and common meditative practices—they can become aware of their breathing. They can speed it up, slow it down, or even in some cases through yogic practices, stop it altogether. The heart is also beating on its own, but it can also be brought under control. All unconscious processes can be brought to the conscious mind, with enough practice. We are doing them already, just not consciously. As an example, Wim Hof, the *Iceman*, has learned how to consciously control his immune system, metabolism, and body temperature, as a result of certain yogic practices. He is widely known for his ability to withstand extreme cold with supernatural ease. This is not a fairytale, it's pretty real, and yogis have been doing it for eons.

Let's simplify the mind into two dimensions:

The conscious dimension, which always comes together with the sense of "I."

For example: "I did that," "I'll go there," "I am sad," "I am joyful," "I am Maverick," etc.

The unconscious dimension, which is always unaccompanied with the sense of "I."

For example, imagine you regularly go to sleep lying on your side with your face pointing toward the right side of the room. However, when you wake up, you are always on your back, with your face pointing up at the ceiling. How did that happen? Did "you" move? Yes, you did, but without the feeling of "I." You probably moved many times in your bed throughout the night, but you performed those actions unaccompanied with the "I-ego," the sense of being an individual. They were "unconsciously" done, as is commonly said.

Is this all there is? No.

There is another "dimension," the dimension of Being, or *superconsciousness*, which just like unconsciousness is not accompanied with the sense of "I," but, in contradistinction, all of the conscious faculties are not only present but also enhanced to an extreme. The "person" is not unconscious, but rather superconscious, above the conscious level, above beyond a "person." That "I-less" state, with no ego, is the state of enlightenment. Some also call it *Samadhi*, but there are many forms of *Samadhi*. They are explained in detail in *The Secret Power of Kriya Yoga*, chapter 18, "The Mysteries of Samadhi Unveiled," for those who are interested.

Superconsciousness	Conscious. No sense of "I," oneness with the whole.
Conscious mind	Conscious. Sense of "I," of an individuality.
Unconsciousness	Unconscious. No sense of "I," like in general anesthesia, faint, deep dreamless sleep, etc.

"Attaining" the superconscious state is not an easy task, not because it "requires arduous spiritual practice through dozens of lifetimes," as is usually said, but because it requires the hardest thing ever: going beyond the person, beyond the personality, beyond "I." The ego is tremendously selfish. Can it ever allow itself go beyond itself? Yes—if its discernment has been awakened and it sees the need of its end.

The ego (individuality) is overrated, anyway. It does not have any real value, and it is the source of all problems and suffering. This sense of separateness creates a multitude of belief systems, dogmas, superiority and inferiority complexes, hate, dissatisfaction, misery, etc. Name anything negative in this world and you can always trace it back to the ego and its preposterous interpretations and thoughts. It is temporary, ever-changing, limited and ever-lacking. It is the moving film in the eternal, unchanging screen of unlimited Consciousness.

Since you need a body to experience the world, body-consciousness and world-consciousness are the same. Even when you do an out-of-body projection or something similar, you still have a body, albeit a subtle one. Whenever the ego-cable is plugged in, connection is made; whenever it is unplugged, connection is lost. It is not even very stable. A simple hit to the head and the body-mind falls unconscious. Such a transient phenomenon is what we usually believe we are.

When someone temporarily loses the "I" in the unconscious state, that person comes back the same. Nothing changed.

When someone consciously dissolves the "I," that "person" does not come back the same. What "comes back" is not even a "person"! New insight, new knowledge and a higher level of awareness that opens the doors of the supreme wisdom, are the result, always accompanied by a joy and peace never known before.[3]

When the egoless state is permanent and effortless, one is truly enlightened. This supreme wisdom is beyond anything the intellect could ever conceive of through logic, reason and

---

[3] Take into consideration that temporary formless Samadhis do not dissolve the "I," they merely deactivate it for some time.

knowledge gathered from the five senses in the conscious state. Reason and the intellect can never take you there. They must and will be transcended. No more will you need to rely on books for knowledge, for your own pure mind can sprout out all the knowledge from the depths of your Consciousness.

Kundalini is what will propel us from our current conscious state to the superconscious state. It is the fuel of the boat that we will use to travel the sea from the cyclical shores of life and death, toward the eternal sands of the Ultimate Reality.

Not only does Kundalini help us reach the peak of supreme existence, but it is also the force underlying every creative and extraordinary act. Depending on the level of your Kundalini awakening, that force may be transmuted into various kinds of expressions. Not only can you awaken supramental faculties, but you can become a brilliant artist, poet, etc. Beautiful music is an expression of this energy. Erwin Schrödinger, a famous scientist in the field of quantum theory and a known reader of the *Upanishads*, used this same creative energy to gain insights into the nature of the cosmos. The examples are countless, but in most of these cases, it is all done unconsciously. Where you focus—there the energy goes. By being attracted to teachings about Kundalini and spirituality, by reading this book and having the noble desire to realize the greatest of human potential, you demonstrate that you already have at least some *Kundalini activation* going on.

Even someone like Napoleon Hill, one of the best known self-help authors in the world (and advisor to U.S. President Woodrow Wilson), talked about transforming "sex energy" into something more productive and worthy. That is because the most potent energy in the human body, if not awakened and raised to higher centers (no matter what kind of expression its output is), will always remain at the gross lower centers and be "wasted" on libido and instinct-driven behaviors.

Have you ever wondered why our culture is based on sex? Sex sells because it is the strongest driving force in humans. It is biologically imprinted in our DNA that reproduction and survival of the species are the most important things a human can do. The vast majority of humans waste their lives and energy on superficial sexual endeavors.

No one starts off with the idea of wanting to awaken their Kundalini to become a superb vehicle of creative or artistic intelligence. In most people, that small level of awakening happens spontaneously or incidentally. Obviously, in this guide, we are going for the ultimate "achievement," which is spiritual enlightenment.

The highest possibility for human beings is to go beyond their self-centeredness and egoism into the divine realm of impersonal and all-pervasive Consciousness-Being.

OVERCOMING ALL OBSTACLES

The obstacles might be many, but they are only there to make you go even faster and deeper into your own being.

Many people want to awaken the Kundalini and have a spiritual life, yet they are not being honest with themselves. They think they are, but they probably aren't.

If you want to awaken the Kundalini and realize your true blissful nature, free from suffering and ignorance, you must surrender your ego-self, commit to your spiritual practice, and listen to the direct and non-dogmatic words of wisdom from someone who has done it before you.

Making up excuses such as "I have no time to practice," will not lead one to everlasting happiness. Besides sincerity, earnestness is a major factor in whether you will "make it," or not. Your desire for the truth must be really intense, above everything else.

Everyone starts with a "monkey mind," so that's not an excuse either. The mind is restless because that's the habit it has cultivated. It's just reaping the fruits it sowed. It now needs proper training and a certain level of attention so that it can, little by little, be brought to one single point of focus. Mind-wandering, drowsiness, and an inability to keep a sustained attention will undoubtedly occur. But they will be overcome.

Eating heavier foods like meat can also have a negative impact on awakening the Kundalini, but vegetarianism is not an absolute requirement. It's merely an aid.

Awakening the Kundalini is not a joke. If done for the wrong reasons, without following proper instructions, or without love and surrenderness, it can backfire. We don't want to end up like Gopi Krishna in his well-known dramatic story, accidentally awakening the Kundalini through one of the side channels rather than the central, bringing catastrophic results[4].

Despite the innumerable obstacles one might face, do not let yourself be hypnotized by the dance of Maya (the illusion of separateness). Always remember to stay true to your heart.

You don't have to surpass all the barriers—you can just drop them.

Imagine you were dreaming. In that dream-life, you wanted to wake up, but there were many apparent obstacles, and you were always busy, never stopping for a moment. You lived your whole life without pausing for a moment. If you had just stopped, you would've woken up.

If you've ever done lucid dreaming, you know that one of the tricks to staying in the dream is to consciously engross

---

[4] *Kundalini: The Evolutionary Energy in Man (1971); Shambhala.*

yourself even more in it. Drown yourself in the dream-senses and you will stabilize your lucid dream (you'll stay asleep). On the other hand, if you stop and do not engage with anything outside of yourself, you will quickly wake up. The same happens here, in what people call "real-life." Sleepwalk through the "rollercoaster of life," and you will not wake up. Fully stop and see the magic happening.

Do not get discouraged with obstacles. Just persevere and be honest with yourself. If you really want it, life will bend before you.

CHAPTER 5

THE ALCHEMY OF THE INSTINCT

Many people talk about celibacy and sex in relation to the awakening of Kundalini. This seems to be a huge taboo, yet sexuality is part of human nature. In the old days, there used to be many rules and restrictions placed upon the practitioners; they had to take monastic vows and be strictly celibate. Hundreds and thousands of years ago, monks abided by this rule.

Nowadays, this seems to be a different story, as we have seen in the last 100 years. Many oriental gurus who came to the West succumbed to the more "liberal behaviors" of western women. They were so used to the rigid and traditional conduct of oriental women that they were seduced by how open sexuality is in western countries in comparison.

The guru can be sexually active, that's not the problem. Sex is part of nature, it is normal. The problem is when the gurus proclaim themselves to be celibate when in fact they are not. That's called deception. Can falsehood be a trait of an enlightened being?

I would never suggest that aspirants impose unnatural rules or restrictions on themselves. Things must be natural. *Brahmacharya* is usually one of the yogic "rules" imposed on practitioners, and everybody thinks it implies celibacy or chastity. Let's see Ramana Maharshi's definition of Brahmacharya:

> "Brahmacharya means 'living in *Brahman*.' It has no connection with celibacy as is commonly understood. A real *brahmachari* finds bliss in *Brahman*, the same as Self."

> - THE TEACHINGS OF RAMANA MAHARSHI (2010)

You are neither your body nor the life-force in it. You are the Consciousness which is prior to both. Of course, in Kriya Yoga, Kundalini Yoga and other kinds of spiritual traditions, we use energy as a means to reach higher states of consciousness.

This means that every time we "save up" our energy so that it can be converted into spiritual energy, instead of expelling it in superficial activities, our *sadhana* (spiritual practice) might go deeper. But this is true only if it is natural! Know that being natural is much better for the body-mind system, and will make your sadhana go deeper than being a forced celibate. Being a forced celibate is one of the worst things you can do on your spiritual path. It will drive you crazy, and the sexual repression will end up diminishing your chances of Self-Realization.

We have to pay attention to the suppression of desires, for they may leave behind latent residues that are not easily erased. Being able to clearly discern why we have those desires, and realizing that their fruit is not better than the bliss within will enable us to drop them without leaving any footprints.

The following quote by H. W. L. Poonja, the known Lucknow Guru, illustrates this perfectly:

"I have traveled to the high altitudes of the Himalayas. In one case I was going on the way to there because I wanted to do as we've heard. After the battle of *Mahabharata*, the *Pandavas* went to heaven by foot. So I also wanted to go by foot. When I arrived at there someone said: 'This way you should go.'

So I started going, and on the way, there was one man doing penance in a cave. He was from Bengal. It was very cold, so I asked him 'Can I spend the night with you?' He said 'Yes, but you must cook.'

It was a very small cave, 6 feet by 6 feet, and he said I would sleep there while he would sleep in the kitchen. There was a stone bench, with a cloth, and the pillow was also made of cloth with sand inside.

So, this man was living in such a sacrifice, but I said 'I don't want this pillow because it's not comfortable. I can sleep without this sand pillow.' When I removed the pillow, under it, I found a book about sex.

So this man had left his country, and went to do penance in the Himalayas and had a *Filmfare* book of sex. So this is the result of going to the caves. If you have to study sex living in such a cold place, why not to stay in your home place?"

- PAPAJI SATSANG IN LUCKNOW, 1994

What's the point of being celibate if your mind is always full of sexual thoughts? Don't fool yourself.

Instead, let's understand this:

There are two instinctive forces in the body-mind which are above all others: The "libido," which is a force related to the reproduction of the species; and the "survival," which is the force related to the preservation of the species. They are both interconnected and take a primal role in the functioning of living beings.

In the case of most humans, when this instinctive impulse and desire arises, humans seem to gain a new invigoration, strength and a sort of a one-pointedness. It stirs up lively effervescence. For example, the presence of an attractive young female, behind closed doors, can seem to disrupt many of the so-called enlightened gurus. Since they have not overcome the most natural impulses, they fall prey to them.[5]

When a baby is born, parents naturally extend their sense of self-preservation toward the child, linking their survival with the child's survival. For example, if a mother has her child trapped under a tree that is humanly impossible to lift, the mother's own survival will appear to be under threat, thus activating her instinct for self-preservation even though her own life is not under any danger. This survival instinct may provide her with "superhuman strength," enabling her to lift the tree and save her child! How many times have we heard stories like that?

Through spiritual practice, these two energies can be harvested and transformed into a higher energy with spiritual purposes. They can also be converted into a super intense desire for Self-Realization. That super intense desire is unlike all other desires because it will burn them all, like a burning log that

---

[5] Again, this is fine as long as the guru is not pretending to be celibate or is not deceiving the student with an "I'll wake up your chakras," or "This tantric session will give you an experience of blissful emptiness" kind-of-stuff.

will consume all the other logs when placed together. That burning desire is the main factor that will determine whether or not you will become liberated. Yes, the intensity of your desire is that important—without it, you will not go far. It is what distinguishes real aspirants from wannabe seekers.

Although many people affirm that Kundalini and sexual energy are the same, that is a just a poor half-interpretation of what it really is. Kundalini is not sexual energy; it is sexual energy that is a low-level partial component of the Kundalini energy. As Kundalini is lying dormant, its "residues" get converted into these two interlinked forces mentioned earlier.[6]

There are also those who, after enjoying countless brief ecstasies from sexual union and ever wanting more, never satisfied with the results that such short joys give, hear about how awakening the Kundalini will prompt a permanent cosmic orgasm. Well, "cosmic orgasm" is not the correct description, although I understand why some say it. Since the ecstasy felt in sexual union is only the tip of the iceberg, when Kundalini awakens and enters into Sushumna, awakening and piercing the lower chakras, lots of sexual-orgasmic-sensations much more powerful than ordinary intercourse will be experienced, which might seem of "cosmic" proportions. Harvesting the sexual energy and transmuting it to a higher purpose can

---

[6] That's why, in enlightened beings, we often see them have indifference toward sexual activity and "body/genes" preservation.

have these side-effects, initially. Yet that is not the purpose of Kundalini awakening—it's just a side effect, which will soon be surpassed if one doesn't hold tightly to such experiences. That can be called "low-level bliss," and is incomparable to the "divine bliss" that is experienced in the higher centers. The higher the energy goes, the more the pleasure and ecstasy will become less "human" or sexual in nature, and more "divine," expanding toward an all-encompassing Oneness.

When this happens, sexual activity and the pleasure derived from it will not seem important to you. If it happens, it happens. The body-mind merely follows its natural course. This is a sure sign that the energy is in the higher centers rather than the lower. The bliss of an orgasm will not be as attractive as it once was, for you want something more profound and everlasting—the bliss of Being.

CHAPTER 6

THE BEGINNING OF UNIVERSALITY

Most experiences will not happen during the practice itself, but in the state afterward, the "post-practice state." They might also occur whenever you are relaxing outside of practice, when you are loosened up and not wanting to do anything in particular. The instant right after waking up or before falling asleep is also great timing for the occurrence of experiences.

With enough practice under your belt, whenever you sit quietly or relax outside of practice, your mind will naturally sink into a tranquil meditative state, and since you are not practicing or doing anything in particular, your consciousness will start to shift from the waking state to the dream state without losing lucidity. It might even go to the deep sleep state, albeit it will do so semi-consciously at first.

One major characteristic of strong experiences is that they

are intentionless, which means you had no intention whatsoever to make them happen—they just did! This shows the importance of letting go of the outcome and of the control-freak named ego.

Although most experiences will not happen during the practice—know that practice is absolutely necessary and the catalyst for everything.[7]

"I have practiced for five months, and nothing happened. Yesterday, I lay on my sofa listening to some *bhajans*, and suddenly I had the most beautiful and expanding blissful experience."—yes, but that was possible because you purified and deepened your mind through spiritual practice during those five months.

Although I often say we have to go beyond experiences, they do still have their place, especially in the beginning. They are big motivators to go further and surrender even more to the Truth, and they can change the course of our lives.

I'll share one that happened to me which changed the course of my spiritual path.

---

[7] Some people have spiritual experiences that occur out of the blue, without having done any practice in this lifetime. Know that they most certainly practiced in some previous life. Usually when these unforeseen experiences happen to a non-meditator, either they think they are mentally crazy, or they recognize something deeper and change their life. Unfortunately, many fall into the trap of trying to recreate them, sinking in a hard-to-overcome abysm.

The sun is intense today. Its light, passing through the window gaps, is capable of waking up even the heaviest sleeper. Becoming aware of the waking state, the mind seems surprisingly alert, yet the body looks like a rock.

A sudden decision arises in me: I'll stay on the bed in the supine position and ride the hypnagogic state.

While drifting in and out of sleep, Anahata's Chakra comes into focus for about 30 seconds—then it is let go for 5 seconds. This creates a mental anchoring in the conscious mind, and even though awareness is going deeper within, unconsciousness will not take hold of me.

It is supposed to be done for smaller and smaller periods of concentration, always increasing the "letting go" time. Many rounds later, 5 seconds concentration, 60 seconds "letting go" is the norm.

Suddenly my consciousness is pulled up and the alertness level goes through the roof. Awareness is pristine in lucidity, even though the physical body consciousness is nearly unheard of.

Massive amounts of energy start to build up in the subtle

body and ecstatic thunderbolts are coming up from the perineum toward the Crown. As soft as a leaf dancing in the wind—but burning with the lightning vibrations of inner fire—that's how I feel.

A rush of pure power resembling a massive explosion in space fiercely goes up through the Sushumna Nadi, not stopping for anything until it reaches the Crown. It's the Kundalini.

My awareness is expanding like a balloon as if the limits of the subtle body are not enough. The expansion is not in a "straight motion," but more like jumping on a trampoline, each time going further and further, enveloping a "huge area," but also coming back to the seeming body-cage. This expansion of consciousness keeps growing and growing until I can no longer recognize where my limits are.

My body is becoming the planet Earth, and every living creature my cells. Joy fills my veins as if my beingness were the creator of life itself. I realize I have never been fully alive before.

The vast Universe has now become my body. It is an all-encompassing infinite vastness. My being is space. I am space... endless space. My identity is no longer limited to a body but pervades the whole cosmos. Everything is in me, but I am also everything. It is clear now that everything is made up of empty space. All atoms, living beings, planets, stars, galaxies, are but empty space. This is all boundless empty space. Yet awareness prevails, not as a normal "I-person," but as an "I-universe," so to speak.

There is no personality, no story, no human traits, not even thoughts. It's an impersonal beingness, just this vast empty space. This unending peace can be found nowhere else but deep inside where silence and joy live together. Everything arises and dissolves in a blink of an eye, being witnessed by this vastness that I am.

Eternity is in my hands. A dance with an unfathomable splendor of unimaginable greatness silently echoes throughout this immeasurable vastness.

Unexpectedly, something alien starts to vibrate. The liberating shock of omnipresence is becoming too much for the mind. A subtle desire of wanting to stay like this forever emerges in my deepest recesses.

"Not yet," a sapient voice says. "An expansion of consciousness is still a movement of the 'I' to the farther limits of mind and matter. You must dissolve the 'I,' and go beyond universality itself."

This voice's wisdom reminds me that I have a name and a story which can't seem to be recollected. The mind feels like a radio ceaselessly searching for a specific frequency until it zaps onto what appears to be the correct memory and individuality.

Blank.

Deep breath. Feel the air fill my lungs. Wow. What just happened? I don't remember anything, yet something *did* happen, only I have no memory of it.

What can only be described as an "extraction" from a "zipped file" occurs, and now I know exactly what happened according to the mind's translation—a cosmic experience.

A rush of joyful energy opens my heart into a universal love. Tears are flowing from my eyes, a consequence of my enormous gratitude for such an amazing experience, which even though it happened just moments ago, it is timeless and present right now.

The sparkling sunlight passing through the windows bursts into my vision. My eyes open. The white ceiling, the dust made visible by the bright sun rays, my heartbeat, whatever is perceived... is part of me. Just like the fingers are one with their hand, just like all dream-forms are one with their dreamer, so every form is One with me.

After that experience, I could feel myself one with every-thing, and although one might think there appeared to be a duality, a separation, there was not. Everything was distinct and could be perceived by the mind's senses, yet at the same time, it was as if I were looking at myself no matter where "I" looked. It was memorable.

When the individual Kundalini is activated and merged with the Cosmic Kundalini, consciousness begins to recognize that it IS beyond the body's limits. You might experience this as an expansion of consciousness, but it is more like a decreasing of a self-contracted consciousness.

Part 2

CHAPTER 7

THE ASCENT OF KUNDALINI

Every morning when you wake up, you become aware of the world. Moments before you were probably in a dream or simply unconscious. Did you ever wonder how this process happens?

A sparkle of impersonal consciousness fires up from the Spiritual Heart, the causal center, up through the finest channel in the subtle body, the *Amrita Nadi*, until it reaches the brain-area. Once it reaches the brain, it gets "transformed" into a personal consciousness, and the I-ego takes form, spreading throughout the whole nervous system. All the excess unneeded power accumulates in the Muladhara Chakra, at the base of the spine.

Even though Consciousness is the Ultimate Reality and the substratum of the whole manifestation, it covers its true nature with the veil of Maya and keeps on externalizing, as dynamic energy, from the Cosmic Kundalini to the individual Kundalini, to the prana that flows through the subtle body.

What we want to do is to gather all the spread-out life-force from all the parts of the nervous system to the central channel in the spine. We will then awaken the latent energy and raise it until it reaches the brain area, and then downward back to where it came. As the Kundalini energy ascends, it passes through all the main chakras in the Sushumna Nadi.

All these practices have the purpose of "working" with your subtle body. The subtle body is the link between matter and consciousness; it is what "binds" consciousness to the body, creating the feeling of "I."

What we will do is unite the upward flowing energy (prana) with the downward flowing energy (apana) which will generate *samana*, a powerful heat-energy in the navel area. This energy is crucial for the awakening of Kundalini. With the main bandhas (locks) and *kumbhaka* (breath-retention), the Kundalini energy will have no chance but to awaken and rise through the central channel.

Restraining the breath is indeed one of the most powerful methods, but I also have to say that it might be considered slightly violent when compared to other techniques. Yet one thing is for certain—it works.

Entering into Sushumna is a question of subtlety and many people say that when they hold their breath for an extended period, their heart rate shoots up and when they resume it, the breath becomes very gross and fast.

This will only happen if you exceed the body's current ability to hold the breath. It must be gentle and relaxing, not a "forcing" that will make you breathe heavily afterward.

If you are panting, you are not doing it correctly. After holding the breath, you must exhale slowly and naturally, and then breathe calmly. Plus, you are supposed to do a breath-holding technique only after you've practiced some other easier form of meditation first, for some time, as a body-mind preparation.

If correctly done, holding the breath in a relaxed manner will instantly make it not only subtler, but also powerfully energetic. Whenever the breath is held, concentration is also much stronger.

Remember, it should always be done prudently and according to the practitioner's present spiritual maturity.[8]

Additionally, doing a technique like Kriya Supreme Fire, where in addition to holding the breath, you also raise the

---

[8] This poses a great question: can you really self-evaluate how "spiritually mature" your mind is? Who is self-evaluating such, the ego? Can you trust it? That's why having the support of an ego-less being is utterly important in such cases.

energy, focus on a particular point, and apply bandhas and mudras, will make the breath even more powerful and subtle. Of course, it will be turbulent in the beginning, but with dedication and practice it should become pretty smooth rather than always being tremendously effortful.

Even something as simple as watching the breath can awaken the Kundalini, but it might take over fifty years. As we know, the speed of your progress depends on your system's capacity, your tolerance to side-effects, your lifestyle, etc. You have to decide for yourself: do you want to proceed faster and have a higher chance of facing some side-effects, or do you want to go progressively, in a gentler way, and have no side-effects? Remember that the spiritual journey is not supposed to be an unpleasant one, but a blissful one. However, how long are you willing to wait to realize what needs no time? How long are you willing to stay asleep, swimming in the ocean of suffering?

CHAPTER 8

THE TRUTH ABOUT SPIRITUAL EXPERIENCES

Sushumna Nadi is the central channel where the fire of the Kundalini energy goes through when it is awakened. It is normally closed, and we will open it by practicing. When we open it, and the Kundalini current goes through it, we go beyond the five senses and enter into higher states of consciousness.

As it goes through each Chakra, many experiences might occur, or conversely, perhaps none will happen. It doesn't matter. Many books expound at length about the different kinds of Kundalini awakening experiences, but this might make practitioners feel depressed if they don't achieve those very same experiences. Know that even if no experience happens, that is perfectly fine and NOT a signal that you aren't progressing. Remember the train example. Many mental signposts are usually given by spiritual books and gurus to help practitioners feel more comfortable on their spiritual journey, but this always creates the feeling of "lacking something."

Stop for a moment.

Let's suppose I told you that the first checkpoint is hearing the cosmic sound of Om.

If you have never heard the Om vibration before, or even if you have, from now on, whether you want it or not, your mind will start to reach out for that experience. In fact, the mind can even trick itself into believing it's experiencing the Om vibration. If you don't experience the cosmic sound of Om, you will think you aren't progressing and that you are failing, which might even cause you to stop practicing and give up your search for Self-Realization.

How many times have these "signposts" eluded practitioners? It is one of the main reasons that many leave "spirituality," or stop "seeking the Truth" or "God." Failing to achieve these *subjective* signposts leads them to make conclusions such as "This is all nonsense;" "It's all fake;" "This spirituality thing is mumbo-jumbo;" "It doesn't work."

I have heard enough of that to be one more who deceives genuine seekers. In the abovementioned example, you might not have heard the Om vibration perhaps because you've already transcended the need for such an experience.

You might go your whole sadhana without ever experiencing anything astonishingly "mystical," and in the last moment, the I-ego dissolves.

You might go your whole sadhana without ever experiencing anything astonishingly "mystical," and the I-ego might never dissolve.

You might go your whole sadhana full of spiritual experiences, and in the last moment, the I-ego dissolves.

You might go your whole sadhana full of spiritual experiences, and the I-ego might never dissolve.

You can never know.

Let me tell you a little secret:

The I-ego wants to preserve itself. If having spiritual experiences keeps it alive and healthy, that's precisely what it will allow you to experience. If, on the other hand, not having any spiritual experience will make you stop trying altogether, then that's what it will attempt to do.

Do you see it?

Having or not having any spiritual experience is not a proper evaluation of your spiritual progress. For all you know, tomorrow you might realize your true ever-present nature!

Progress may be indiscernible to the practitioner. The mind going all over the place might be a sign of progress. How do you know? There are countless cases of people starting to practice and having the usual "monkey mind." After one year of practicing, their mind is now peaceful every time they do their sadhana. One day, they sit down to practice and the mind scatters in a way that they've never experienced before. Now, every time they meditate, the mind is absolutely uncontrollable. They don't understand... what's going on? Let me tell you that this might actually be a sign of progress! There are cases that, when you hit a certain threshold of depth in your practice, the ego will attempt anything to disrupt you. It knows its end might be near!

Never get discouraged, and *know* that if you are practicing the correct practices (as I have been sharing since Book 1) with true surrender and intent, then you'll undoubtedly make it all the way to the "end."

Always remember: never practice to achieve any particular outcome, but because you enjoy and love practicing. It's a moment of joy and peace. Whatever is meant to happen will happen, and it will be for your good. Be persistent and go all the way. Nobody ever regretted being enlightened. It's the ultimate goal of every living being, even if they don't know it yet.

BEYOND THE THREE KNOTS

It is said in yogic literature that there are three main knots (*granthis*) in the subtle body, located along Sushumna Nadi, and that they must be untied in order to allow the energy to go through, otherwise they will keep strengthening the sense of "I am this body." These knots are energetic and emotional blockages reinforced by negative experiences and impressions, and they create a firm obstruction to the movement of the life-force.

Doing spiritual practices and self-investigation will progressively untie them, making all the stored up latent impressions come to the surface so that we can erase them altogether.

Contrary to popular belief, our mind is not wholly in the head, but rather is spread out through the body, sometimes even expanding beyond it. Traumas, fears, and all emotional contractions and repressions are stored in the appropriate energetic place within the subtle body. Even small things like a foot massage or practicing some specific asanas, if correctly done, can relieve one of emotional stressors that have been stored up.

As the spiritual practice progresses, Sushumna will not feel like a "tube" with "vortexes of energy," "chakras" or "knots" in it anymore, but rather like a completely hollow tube.

Sometimes, you will not even be able to discern any chakra whatsoever, as if they have merged and only space can be perceived.

Anyway, we will take an entirely different approach and disregard all that. The only thing we gain by acquiring such knowledge is intellectual grandiosity or mental confusion. It's sufficient to know that by doing the correct practice, we will remove all the blockages, especially their root—the knot of ignorance.

CHAPTER 9

KUNDALINI SADHANA

First of all, I want to make one thing clear:

Don't believe anything anyone says, not even this book. Whoever asks you to believe in something blindly does not have your best interests in mind. You must directly experience in your meditation what this book is teaching.

Direct experience is our true teacher. We may reason and talk the talk, but if we don't walk the walk, we will never cut it. You will never know the city of Bethlehem by seeing some photographs or reading about it in a travel guide. These things can spur the curiosity in you, but you must go there and know it by yourself.

Since this book can also be read on its own without having read the previous two, I will briefly give some beginner's tips: before we go into any spiritual practice or meditation, the first lesson is just to sit and let the mind do its thing. Many people have the belief that they control their minds. What a surprise when they sit for the very first time and their mind runs them over, entirely uncontrolled.

If you think you are in control, I suggest you sit for ten minutes and have no thoughts. Can you do it? If you are in control, then no thoughts will occur. If you aren't... you know what will happen. Many thoughts and images can come up, some might even be horrible, but don't worry. They are not really "your" thoughts. Your mind is like a radio, and it can tune into different kinds of energy. Don't pay attention to any of that. The more you practice, the less control the mind will have over you.

When you first start practicing, even the sound of a falling leaf will seem like an explosion. Your mind is getting used to consciously perceiving the subtler elements of the Universe. Again, don't pay any attention to any distractions, let them come and go.

Many gurus share a multitude of techniques, making things seem more complicated than they actually are. Only the practices that produce the strongest results in the shortest amount of time should be chosen. I don't care from which tradition they came. Egotistical gurus praise their traditions while attacking all others. We take what works and drop what doesn't. Our energetic practices have the purpose of awakening and raising the Kundalini—that's our only criteria when picking them. One should always keep an open mind and give an honest attempt to the chosen practice before jumping to any conclusions. That might mean six months of practice, not two weeks. If you don't practice, this whole book will be nothing more than intellectual entertainment.

While Kriya Yoga is generally a softer, gentler approach, the Kundalini Yoga shared here is more "brute-force[9]." One is not better than the other, they are just slightly different approaches with the same goal. For example, I always advise Kriya Yoga practitioners to do the Supreme Fire technique in conjunction with Pranayama, Maha Mudra and Khechari Mudra, as it is a more balanced overall approach. On the other hand, it also needs more effort and time, which many can't afford. Since this is a Kundalini book, I will abstain from sharing classic Kriya Yoga techniques here. Instead, I'll focus on the most powerful Kundalini awakening method and optional auxiliary practices that support it.

In the previous books I've mentioned prana and bandhas, but many people still have questions regarding both, although I'm not keen on profoundly exploring such themes. The reason is that such knowledge is not a requirement for Self-

---

[9] It's not the same as the known Yogi Bhajan's "Kundalini Yoga."

Realization. It can also get excessively esoteric, and while there's nothing wrong with that, it might be a slight detour from our simple, ultimate goal. With that being said, I will give a direct explanation about their purpose in the context of our spiritual practice and Kundalini awakening.

DEMYSTIFYING PRANA

Prana means vital-force or life-force, and it is subdivided into five main types: Prana Vayu[10], Apana Vayu, Samana Vayu, Udana Vayu and Vyana Vayu.

When a practitioner through yogic practices merges the inspired and expired breaths (Prana and Apana Vayus respectively), which are usually out of balance, they neutralize each other. When both airs are neutralized, a single air known as Samana[11] emerges in the abdominal region around the navel area. This energy/air is imperative for the awakening and rising of the Kundalini. That's why we address the navel region with Kriya Supreme Fire. Samana will then gradually

---

[10] Although "prana" is one of the subdivided types, it is also the name given to the collective term of all life-force. I use "prana vayu" for the subdivision and "prana" as the collective term. "Vayu" means "air" or "wind."

[11] One of the translations for Samana is "together," "pacified" (sam) and "air" or "breath," (an/ana) which we can work out to "pacified breath" or "airs together." Now we know why it is called Samana.

awaken the dormant Shakti in the root, transforming into Udana, the "ascending air" or "vertical breath," which rises from that low center to the higher centers. After going through the Chakras and reaching the highest one, it will convert into Vyana, the "omnipresent" or "all-pervading" air. Normally, this air pervades the whole body, but following the course and transformations mentioned above, it permeates the entire universe rather than just an individual body.

Prana, the dynamic energy, is what gives life to what would otherwise be insentient. It is related both to the breath, which is a gross manifestation of prana, and to the mind, which can be said to be subtle prana.

Establishing control of prana is extremely important in spiritual practices because it is the intermediary between the breath and the mind. The breath is easy to take conscious control of, contrary to the mind, which is equated with a monkey, being habitually capricious, uneasy, and volatile. Just like you can control the monkey with a chain, you can control the mind with the breath, especially when you hold it.

Have you ever noticed that when you are extremely concentrated on something, your breath momentarily comes to a stop?

When the breath is restrained, the mind's activities slow down and eventually stop. When there are no thoughts, all the energy is powerfully brought to its source, the Spiritual Heart, where everything will dissolve. Yogis have taken advantage of the knowledge regarding the connection between life-force, breath and the mind for millennia. That's how techniques such as Pranayama were created.

We will also take advantage of this knowledge and apply one main technique that is in truth the agglomeration of many techniques.

THE POWER OF BANDHAS

Bandhas are a fundamental technique in awakening the Kundalini. Seeing that yoga has been distorted to the extent of people competing in international "asana-fitness" contests, doing headstands, the lotus posture and the abdominal lock (*Uddiyana Bandha*) all at the same time, some honest practitioners, whose intention is real Freedom and not physical prowess, have prematurely considered simple techniques like bandhas to be worthless. They are in fact the opposite of uselessness; do not let their simplicity fool you. Although they are not enough on their own, when used as an add-on to other techniques, especially those involving breath-retention, they make a tremendous difference.

Bandha means "body lock." A specific part of the body is firmly but gently contracted, which will have a direct effect on the subtle body. These locks prevent prana from escaping, thus helping to sustain a higher level of energy that can be directed upward. They are also potent Kundalini stimulators and can even improve blood flow and physical health by massaging the internal organs and nerves.

By practicing these bandhas with breath retention, the body will heat up immensely, which with the addition of a precise point of concentration, will have a tremendous impact on awakening the Kundalini.

The three bandhas we will use are *Mula Bandha, Uddiyana Bandha*, and *Jalandhara Bandha*. Together they make up the *Maha Bandha*, the "Great Lock."

1. Mula Bandha
(Perineum Lock)

Many esoteric explanations can be given to Mula Bandha, but it's just a name for the contraction of the perineum, which is the area between the scrotum and the anus in males, and between the vulva and the anus in females.

It is straightforward to do. Focus on the perineum and contract the muscles there. That's it, pretty easy.

If for some reason you lack the mind-muscle connection to do it, do not worry. That's not a problem. You can easily accomplish it within a few days of various attempts.

To hasten this process, you can work on your pelvic muscles. Lay down on your back and pump those muscles for as long as you can while letting the rest of the body relax. After some days or weeks, you will be able to consciously control these muscles.

When sitting cross-legged, if you can press the perineum with the heel while doing this bandha, it will help stimulate Muladhara Chakra and Sushumna itself.

In our practice, we will do this bandha together with two mudras, *Vajroli / Sahajoli Mudra* and *Ashwini Mudra*, for an even more potent effect.

Mudra means "seal." It is a gesture performed to improve the flow of the subtle energies. Despite being associated with hand gestures, they can be done with any part of the body or even the whole body.

Vajroli / Sahajoli Mudra (sexual organ contraction)

Vajroli Mudra is for men, while Sahajoli Mudra is for women. They both do the same thing, but they are slightly different since both sexes have different anatomies. I'll give you a raw and straightforward explanation of how to do them: just hold the same muscles you hold when you want to stop urinating. This sentence makes everyone quickly understand how to do it. In our case, it is okay if you can't hold the perineum and the urethral sphincter separately because we want to hold both at the same time.

Ashwini Mudra (anal contraction)

Ashwini Mudra is done by contracting the anal sphincter. Again, in this particular case, it's okay if you can't do it by itself separately since we'll be using both mudras and Mula Bandha at the same time.

With enough practice, you will be able to firmly apply Mula Bandha, Vajroli/Sahajoli Mudra, and Ashwini Mudra while you are holding the breath for a long time.

These three techniques are also excellent to sublimate sexual energy and raise it to the higher centers.

Remember that from now on, whenever I refer to Mula Bandha in this book, it is actually the combination of Mula Bandha, Vajroli / Sahajoli Mudra, and Ashwini Mudra, as explained, just for simplicity.

There will come a time when doing a single Mula Bandha will activate the Kundalini energy upward, producing immense bliss from the Root to the Crown. The whole Sushumna Nadi will be ecstatically and vibrantly perceived.

2. Uddiyana Bandha
(Abdominal Lock)

Suck your abdomen in and upward. Hold that contraction. That's it. In our practice, we will do this bandha while holding the air inside. It is best you do it when the stomach is empty.

This technique stimulates the Manipura Chakra, arousing a lot of heat and fire in that area. It will also excite the sympathetic nerves of the so-called "solar plexus region," bringing many health benefits.

Although it might be slightly challenging to do it while we are retaining the air inside, due to the inability of the diaphragm to go up as far when our lungs are full of air, with time and practice we will learn how to do it with ease.

3. Jalandhara Bandha
(Chin lock)

Gently bend the head forward and press the chin against the top of the sternum. That's all you have to do. Be careful with your neck and do the movement slowly.

This bandha stops prana from leaving the body in the throat area and often helps to improve the flow of Kundalini there, which practitioners often report to be semi-blocked.

Due both to the contraction of the thyroid and the pressure of the chin on the top of the sternum, the latter of which regulates blood flow in that area, your metabolism and heartbeat might slow down, bringing more relaxation.

If you have problems with your cervical spine, perhaps you shouldn't use this technique. Keeping it safe is always a smart move.

THE BEST KUNDALINI AWAKENING TECHNIQUE

To obtain more aliveness and contentment in our daily lives, and ultimately, the absolute bliss of true enlightenment, we need to practice a method that directly arouses the Kundalini energy.

There are many ways to do it, and throughout the years I have found five powerful "technical" details that seem to affect it the most. In no particular order:

Breath-retention — Mula Bandha — Uddiyana Bandha — Muladhara Chakra Focus — Sahasrara Chakra Focus.

Using any of these methods in your spiritual practice will boost your chance of awakening the Kundalini. They will also increase the heat in your body, which directly influences the awakening of Kundalini. It is no wonder that several traditions call it *Agni* or "inner fire."

This is why we will practice a technique called Kriya Supreme Fire—because it incorporates many of the methods aforementioned, and it generates a tremendous fire in the belly region. Out of all the practices I have done, Kriya Supreme Fire or a similar variant was the most powerful to awaken the Kundalini, and consequently to experience the supreme ecstasy of Samadhi. It is not, however, recommended for beginners.

For those who have already read Kriya Yoga Exposed or The Secret Power of Kriya Yoga:

If you practice as taught there, or are fully happy with your current sadhana, you can either skip this section or keep reading to refresh your memory with the practical details and information regarding Kriya Supreme Fire, plus some new auxiliary practices and instructions.

Kriya Supreme Fire

We will use a variation of this technique that I shared in the Kriya Yoga books of this *Real Yoga Series*, but with a slightly different emphasis on some explanatory details, as this is a book on Kundalini. It is far more potent than traditional spiritual techniques as you will discover for yourself. A myriad of spiritual wealth will be in your hands.

It is a straightforward method, efficient, and easy to do. You don't have to assume or believe in anything. You practice and get the results. It will be obvious. This practice is especially suitable for those who always say: "I never feel anything in my meditations."

Once you become proficient at practicing this technique, you will know that no other energetic practice is needed; this is enough to take care of the "Shakti/Energy/Mother/Bliss" part. For the "Shiva/Consciousness/Father/Wisdom" part, we will *do* something else.

The energy and bliss generated will be so strong that you won't have to force yourself to come back to practice every day. It will not be a chore, but a joy. With time and proper practice, your mind will have no desire to do anything else, since the bliss experienced in your meditation will give it total satisfaction.

First of all, you need to be able to hold your breath between 1 minute 30 seconds and 2 minutes. If you still can't do at least 1 minute and 30 seconds, then you should do the preliminary practice throughout the day. Try to hold the breath for as long as you can but do not tighten up the body. Instead, attempt to keep it relaxed, avoiding too much pressure. Retain the breath only as long as is comfortable; overdoing it may cause lung issues. Do not neglect this recommendation.

Gradually increase the time without undue strain until you can reach between 1 minute 30 seconds and 2 minutes. Use a timer to know precisely how long you can hold it for.

Useful guidelines for the preliminary practice:

#1 Don't do it with a full stomach, as this practice will actively wake up the huge fire in your belly region.

#2 You can do it sitting in your meditation posture, before your current spiritual practice, or whenever you can throughout the day. Do not do it while driving or in any situation that might be dangerous.

#3 Inhale only up to 80%-90% lung capacity and hold until you can do more than 1 minute 30 seconds smoothly. Do not exceed your capacity. Go with ease.

#4 The point of attention should be in the navel zone.

#5 It might take some days or weeks to be able to hold the breath for the stipulated time with ease, and that is fine. Be gentle and not in a hurry.

#6 You will probably sweat a lot, and your body might shake and heat up. That is normal. Just don't faint and don't exceed your current ability. It will increase with practice.

#7 If the fear of death or choking comes up, but internally you are still feeling at ease, even in the midst of such a situation, you can keep going. If not, or if you feel like you are definitely going to faint, it is better to stop. Sometimes a feeling of being spaced-out happens, and that's okay.

#8 Do not let your head get too hot. The whole body should be warm and comfortable.

This is a simple preparatory practice. Just focus on your navel, inhale and hold the breath until you can do it *comfortably* for the stipulated time.

Details

This practice is powerful, so please go easy. Do not go above your ability. Slow and steady wins out over fast and uncontrolled.

The concentration spot should be either in the navel zone, 3-4 fingerbreadths below the navel, on the perineum, or in the heart space. Try each one and see which one fits you best. Always maintain a straight spine and never allow your body to bend.

At the beginning of this practice, you might feel a lot of heat, then you might start shaking or having some sort of mini-convulsions, and finally, a massive empty silence will fill you up. The sheer amount of energy built up with this practice is immense. Often, the heat generated will gradually lead to ecstatic feelings that strongly grab your attention.

However, there might be uncomfortable side-effects as well, including rage, impatience in daily life, pain in the body, itching in the legs, headaches, insomnia, etc., but there can also be an increase in appetite, and a boost in self-confidence, willpower, and vital-energy. Above all, you might finally be able to clearly feel the Pranic/Kundalini energetic-currents. If you get too angry or enraged, or if things aren't going well, you should slow down for a while. You can practice a simple Pranayama or just witness the in-breath and the out-breath until you are ready to attempt Kriya Supreme Fire again after some days.

You can try to do this practice on its own, but doing it with Pranayama and Mahamudra (as explained in the Kriya Yoga books) might help you lessen the side-effects.

When this practice opens your subtle central channel and the

Kundalini starts moving inside of it, unimaginable bliss will be experienced. All the pleasures you experienced in life prior to this point will feel meaningless in comparison to such bliss and joy.

Instructions

1- Touch the soft palate with your tongue, and keep it there throughout the entire practice (if you can do Khechari Mudra as is taught in Kriya Yoga, do it).

2- Inhale up to 75-90% full capacity, pulling the energy up from the Root Chakra (Muladhara) toward the Heart Chakra (Anahata).

3- Hold the breath, gently, and pull your lower abdomen in and up, and lock it firmly as in Uddiyana Bandha with Mula Bandha and Jalandhara Bandha as well. Keep all three locks until you exhale.

4- Relax and hold the breath for about two minutes, if possible in the heart area instead of the belly area.

5- Focus on your chosen concentration spot. Choose where it feels empty and spacious (navel, 3 or 4 fingers below, perineum or the heart space).

6- You will feel a massive heat and will probably be shaking, but then... a vast silence comes. Stay with that silence for as long as you can, but don't go over the prescribed two minutes.

7- Release everything and exhale. Notice how the Heart Chakra opens and joy is felt afterward. You might also feel some "ecstatic electricity" going from the Root Chakra upward through the spinal column.

8- Relax and calm down.

If this is not the first time you practice meditation, do Kriya Supreme Fire up to three times for the first couple of weeks. Then you can increase it as much as you want, as long as you feel comfortable. Some people do it for as much as half an hour to a full hour. It depends on how much time you've devoted to the practice and on your system's capacity.

Go slowly with regards to how much time you do this practice for. Your system will start to adapt in as little as one month, provided you do it every day with full dedication. Each round doesn't take much time to do, but if properly done, the effects are powerful.

Kriya Supreme Fire will burn lots of energetic blockages, and although it is a powerful practice, by having practiced the breath retention preliminaries and the other auxiliary spiritual practices like Pranayama or Breath-Witnessing, plus some grounding activity, it will not feel too demanding for your system.

It is critical that you are proficient at and already capable of correctly executing the three main bandhas as mentioned previously.

Your life-force will be building up already, and if you have not yet awakened the Kundalini, bandhas will be the key. They are very important, but usually take a secondary role in many spiritual practices.

This practice is a powerful bomb to awaken the primal energy. The intense pressure and heat waves will shake the dormant Kundalini into awakening, fiercely going up through the Sushumna Nadi.

You should do it twice a day, first in the morning and then later in the evening. If sleeplessness comes to you, don't do it near bedtime, but before dinner. If too much energy builds up, you might need to do some "grounding work."

Between each round, you can repose for some time (30 seconds or even 1 to 2 minutes) in the after-effect. Then proceed to do another round.

Remember the symptoms' levels we talked earlier in the book? If you practice Kriya Supreme Fire for one hour, it's a full level 10. Doing the Crown techniques and Khechari Mudra as explained in *The Secret Power of Kriya Yoga*, with Kriya Supreme Fire for at least 30 minutes is also a level 10.

This practice is mainly about focus. If you can use your power of concentration to do it as correctly as possible, it will be successful. Usually, lots of distracting thoughts will arise such as "I have to do this," "I need to go eat," "I need to finish some papers" or "I need to check my email." These would typically prevent you from having a good practice session. However, by applying all the bandhas and by utilizing the breath-retention method during this practice, the mind will be forced to be quiet. Afterward, the pleasurable sensations you start feeling will help to effortlessly keep it serene. Since the breath, the life-force and the mind are all interrelated, each one being the subtler aspect of the former, when we control the breath, we control the life-force, and we end up controlling the mind.

You should also practice in the same place, at the same time, every day. Your mind will get used to practicing at that time, in that environment, and it will be significantly easier to go into the "meditative state" right from the beginning. When "entering" into such a mind-state becomes second nature, induced only by the act of sitting to practice, you can then practice anytime, anywhere.

Sometimes, the bliss and heat might be so intense that you temporarily lose consciousness. That's okay. As soon as you "come back," keep doing what you were doing. Remember to not force anything, for the movement of the Kundalini current should be gentle, subtle and naturally blissful, although often, the first time it rises, it is more like an explosion.

During the practice, you might start getting afraid of dying. What happens is that when this method gets really strong, it slightly simulates death. You have to discern here; if you are going above your capacity, stop. Again, be gentle and do not rush. If you've experienced this before and know that nothing serious will happen to you, keep going. Usually, the worst that can happen is that you faint and wake up moments later, but it's preferable that you don't go this far.

It might occur, subsequently, that after the end of your practice, you enter into a Self-Awareness state which is not like your typical day-to-day awareness. It's like a blissful heightened awareness of "just being." When this happens, stay as long as you can in this state. It is magical and the best state to clear all your tendencies, desires, *karma, samskaras, vasanas*, predispositions, etc. It is a prelude to the enlightenment beingness state—a natural, effortless, empty non-dual bliss awareness. If this "state" happens, not at the end, but during the practice, or during any moment of the day, let go of everything and melt in it[12]! It's such a blessing, and when it naturally starts happening more and more, you know you are unlocking a huge door toward Freedom.

---

[12] If you are driving, or anything like that, do not do it. Be responsible and safe.

The combination of this Kundalini awakening practice, along with the state you get afterward, the post-practice Self-Awareness state (other traditions may refer to it as *Parvastha*, Background Witness or Presence of Being) is the main catalyst for the awakening of profound non-dual wisdom.

Crown Variant

In Kriya Supreme Fire, practitioners normally place their attention on either the perineum, the heart, the navel or 3 to 4 fingers below the navel. This will work fine for the majority of practitioners. Yet, for some, placing their attention on the Crown Chakra is a better alternative, being a super powerful Kundalini magnet. With this in mind, here's a variation of Kriya Supreme Fire for those interested in the so-called "dangerous yet blissful" Crown focus:

Instructions for the Crown Supreme Fire

1- Touch the soft palate with your tongue, and keep it like that throughout the entire practice (if you can do Khechari Mudra as is taught in Kriya Yoga, do it).

2- Inhale up to 75-90% full capacity, pulling the energy up from the Root Chakra (Muladhara) toward the Crown Chakra (Sahasrara).

3- As you inhale, apply the Crown *Shambhavi Mudra*. Roll

your eyes upward toward the Crown, comfortably. It is as if you were attempting to look at the ceiling. Do not move your head or close your eyes, let them be semi-opened. They might blink a lot at the beginning, but with practice, it will be natural. Just don't strain them. This mudra will collect all the prana in the Crown Chakra.

4- Hold the breath, gently, and pull your lower abdomen in and up, and lock it firmly as in Uddiyana Bandha with Mula Bandha. Keep both locks until you exhale. *Do not* apply Jalandhara Bandha.

5- Focus all your attention on the Crown Chakra. Relax and keep the breath held for about two minutes.

6- Release everything and exhale. Notice how ecstatic your whole body is. The "sensations" can go from a warm pleasure-feeling to a super intense "out of control" bliss.

8- Relax and calm down.

The effects will be slightly different from the typical Kriya Supreme Fire, but the overall chance of having side-effects will be similar if not higher. The Crown Chakra is a very sensitive "place," and it all depends on the practitioners' body-capacity. There is a very high chance you will feel spaced-out if you are not used to focusing on the Crown Chakra, as if you were "high." Go slowly and prudently.

Auxiliary Practices

These are practices for those who are not yet ready to practice Kriya Supreme Fire in its entirety. They are optional, and a suggested routine will be given at the end.

Breath-Witnessing

Breath meditation is a great straightforward beginner's practice. Sit cross-legged or in a chair and breathe naturally for some rounds. After 4-5 breaths, slow down your breathing and witness the in-breath, the natural pause, and the out-breath. This is extremely peaceful, and your heart rate and metabolism will rapidly slow down. Then, let go of trying to control the breathing. That's it. Just keep witnessing the inhalations, pauses, and exhalations, without ever forcing the breathing. Although you were the one slowly inhaling and exhaling at the beginning, after some minutes you will notice the breath is going by itself; you don't have to do anything, only witness it.

If you get lost in thought, once you recognize that you're not paying attention to the breath, just come back. If at some point you start seeing something that resembles either a sun/bright yellowish circle or a moon/bright whitish circle, you can begin witnessing that instead of the breath. Many meditations follow along these lines, but we are practicing this technique only to get a firm base of concentration, not to follow mental signposts. It doesn't matter if anything appears or does not appear since this is merely a preparation for stronger practices.

If you prefer, you can do Kriya Pranayama as taught in *Kriya Yoga Exposed* instead. It is a stronger practice, but also slightly more complex.

Sushumna Pranayama

This practice is more advanced than Breath-Witnessing. Its purpose is to help us locate Sushumna Nadi and to develop our concentration further, although it is still a preparation to improve the system's capacity. If you practice any other kind of Pranayama already, you can keep doing it. Since Kriya Supreme Fire is only done 3 times in the beginning, we still need to add another practice after it to help our system improve its pranic capability faster.

Sit cross-legged or in a chair.

1- Mentally chant Om focused on Muladhara Chakra, applying Mula Bandha at the same time.

2- Right after applying Mula Bandha, inhale using *ujjayi* breathing (ocean breathing) raising the energy from the Root

(Muladhara Chakra) to the center of the head (Ajna Chakra) through the middle of the spinal cord. The energy should not go through the front, the back or the middle of the body, but through the middle of the spinal cord, which is where Sushumna Nadi is. Locate it the best you can.

3- As soon as the energy reaches Ajna Chakra, chant Om there focused on Ajna.

4- Take a natural pause for about one second.

5- Chant Om focused on Ajna and exhale all the way down through Sushumna Nadi until the energy reaches Muladhara Chakra again. As soon as you start exhaling, let go of Mula Bandha and slowly apply Uddiyana Bandha. Suck your abdomen in and upward, which will culminate in having the whole abdominal region sucked in by the time you have no more air to exhale, as if you wanted to merge the navel with the spine.

6- When there is no more air to expel, and the energy has reached the Root, chant Om focused on Muladhara and let go of Uddiyana Bandha, allowing a natural pause of about one second.

This is one round. You can do any number of rounds during the stipulated time.

Although it might seem complex, it's simple. You are applying Mula Bandha only when inhaling and raising the energy, while applying Uddiyana Bandha only when exhaling and moving the energy down. You'll be mentally chanting Om every time you reach the top and the bottom, right before making a small natural pause.

Mantra Meditation

Mantra meditation is said to be superior to breathing meditation because once we get deep enough, the external breathing might stop altogether, leaving us with no object of meditation, which doesn't happen with a mantra-based practice. Obviously, this does not mean that a breath-based practice is a dead-end, but that a shift into subtler objects of meditation will naturally happen as we get better at it, such as the mental image of the breath, inner sounds, inner lights, and so on. These subtle objects will automatically "appear" either when the breath gets very subtle, or when it stops completely.

With that said, mantra meditation by itself without a focus point seems to be imbalanced for many sensitive practitioners; hence it's usually put together with a breathing meditation. What often happens is that earlier on, you will get fantastic results, but after 6-12 months of practice, the adverse side-effects of practicing a mantra-based meditation exclusively, without "placing it" in a particular body-point, will creep up, overloading your subtle body.

Since we are only using it as an auxiliary or preparatory practice for Kriya Supreme Fire, it will be fine. Additionally, many aspirants report tremendous success with it, without any problematic side-effects, even in the long run.

I will not give you a specific mantra because it always depends on your predispositions, and mental and devotional tendencies. Some practitioners will do better with the universal *Om*, or *I am*, others with a *bija mantra* (*Ram*, *Lam*, etc.) or their chosen *Ishta-Devata* (personal God) mantra. Usually, shorter mantras are better for this kind of practice, rather than a longer one.

Sit cross-legged or in a chair. Mentally chant your chosen mantra. You can place it on the navel region, the Heart, or in the middle of the head. Whenever you lose your attention, just come back to the mantra and the selected focus point. You can either do it for a full *mala* (108 repetitions) or for 20 minutes. That's it.

There are a lot of details and precision behind all these auxiliary practices when they are the central practice, but since they are only auxiliary in this case, we don't have to burden ourselves with such details. We will keep them simple, so that they do precisely what we want them to do—prepare the ground for Kriya Supreme Fire.

Suggestions for a Kundalini Yoga Routine

You should choose the level that fits your system's capacity. If you've been practicing for a long time, you can start with the Advanced Intermediate stage and see how it goes. If you are an absolute beginner, I suggest you start by practicing a simple "witnessing the breath" meditation for 20 minutes a day before doing the practice taught in this book. You can also practice Kriya Yoga, as it is better suited for those prone to over sensitivity.

Beginners shouldn't begin with Kriya Supreme Fire due to a high likelihood of having less than welcome side-effects. Starting with auxiliary practices will help them prepare the subtle body, and then when it's ready and the mind is calmer and more mature, they can slowly incorporate Kriya Supreme Fire into their sadhana.

Beginner:

- Mula Bandha for 50 contractions as instructed.

- Kriya Supreme Fire preliminary practice to gain breath-restraining capacity.

- Breath-Witnessing for 20 minutes or Mantra Meditation for 108 times using a mala or for 20 minutes.

- After finishing, stay for 2 to 5 minutes in the "post-practice state." If thoughts, memories, emotions, etc., come up, just witness them and realize that since you are observing them, they cannot be you. They are outside of you, the witness. Remain as that.

Another option is to practice Kriya Yoga as shared in Kriya Yoga Exposed without doing Kriya Supreme Fire.

Practice twice a day, preferably in the morning and before dinner. It is imperative that you develop a regular meditation practice, overcoming procrastination and impatience for results. Although distractions will make you forget your object of meditation, with enough practice you will shorten the periods of "lost in thought." Stay lucid and avoid falling asleep.

When you've been consistent with your mediation for at least three months, can do Mula Bandha pretty easily, sustain the attention on the breath or mantra for minutes with minimal mind-wandering, and are comfortable restraining your breath for a minimum of 90 seconds, you can go to the Intermediate phase.

Intermediate:

- Kriya Supreme Fire 3 times.

- Breath-Witnessing or Sushumna Pranayama for 20 minutes or Mantra Meditation for 108 times using a mala or for 20 minutes.

- Post-practice state for 5-10 minutes.

Another option is to practice Kriya Yoga as shared in Kriya Yoga Exposed with Kriya Supreme Fire or practice Kriya Bow instead of Kriya Supreme Fire until you feel more prepared, as shared in The Secret Power of Kriya Yoga.

Practice twice a day, preferably in the morning and before dinner.

When you've been consistent with your meditation for about six months, rarely losing your object of attention, not getting distracted by either thoughts (even if they pose as intellectual insights) or outside events, can do Kriya Supreme Fire without "forcing," and are comfortable restraining your breath for 120 seconds—you can go to the Advanced Intermediate phase. Make sure you do not confuse sharp, lucid attention with dull second-rate peripheral focus.

Advanced Intermediate:

- Kriya Supreme Fire for 15 to 20 minutes.

- Post-practice state 15 to 20 minutes.

Another option is to practice Kriya Yoga as shared in Kriya Yoga Exposed with Kriya Supreme Fire for 15-20 minutes, reducing Kriya Pranayama to 36 or 72 breaths.

Practice twice a day, preferably in the morning and before dinner.

At this point, we let go of our auxiliary practices, for now we already have a sufficiently tranquil focused mind, and breath-retention power capable of proficiently performing Kriya Supreme Fire. Breath-retention and bandhas will be a tremendous help in preventing subtle distractions from overcoming our one-pointed attention during the practice. Although Kriya Supreme Fire is done with continuous full-effort, the "post-state" is semi-effortlessly abided in, being much stronger than what was previously experienced.

In this state, a degree of vigilance might still be needed, but a "letting go" must start to be the primary "activity" you "do." Different kinds of Samadhis will also start to occur, e.g., you might perceive inner light, inner sound, lots of non-physical full-blown experiences, periods of ecstatic joy, etc. During those moments, you can sit for hours without discomfort or distractions.

Then, throughout the subsequent months, if you are side-effect free, you can slowly increase up to 30-60 minutes of Kriya Supreme Fire and 20-30 minutes of post-practice "just being."

After many months, at least six, maybe more, depending on how you feel and how ready you are (external help is useful to evaluate how spiritually mature you are), you can come up to the point of doing one hour of Kriya Supreme Fire and 30 minutes of "just being." It depends on how powerful each Kriya Supreme Fire round is. One full hour is absurdly powerful, and if each round brings you to a massive post-practice state of bliss consciousness already, then you probably don't need to do many.

Advanced:

When your Kundalini has already fully awakened, and you can get into a powerful bliss/Samadhi state by practicing a small amount of Kriya Supreme Fire, then you should practice exactly that amount, followed by abiding in Self-Awareness the rest of the time. This is the most important state to erase all karma, tendencies, and desires.

- Kriya Supreme Fire 1-60 minutes.

- Post-practice state 30-60 minutes.

Another option is to practice Kriya Yoga as shared in The Secret Power of Kriya Yoga, but with special attention to the Kriya's Parvastha state of just being.

Practice twice a day.

When you can drop all effort and still maintain an unbroken

blissful Self-Awareness state, empty of everything besides bliss, then you can proceed to the final stage.

No-practice Stage:

At this point, it doesn't matter if it's formally sitting or whatever you are doing throughout the day—your practice is to stay aware of being, of "I am," being consciously present throughout the whole day. It's like the "post-practice Self-Awareness state" but lasting the whole day, effortlessly.[13]

Or "Expanding Parvastha" from The Secret Power of Kriya Yoga

These are only suggestions, not rules and you should see which kind of practices and schedule fit you better. It always depends on your level of spiritual ripeness and how much time and motivation you have. In general, a Kundalini/energetic practice and a Consciousness/beingness practice will be enough. It doesn't need to be overcomplicated, just straightforward and potent.

---

[13] Do not do it in a dangerous situation that demands your full attention, like operating heavy machinery.

Breath-Retention

There are some practitioners whose bodies might be unable to sustain the breath for long periods of time due to health concerns. This means they will be unable to practice Kriya Supreme Fire, as breath-retention is one of its vital components.

With that being said, many people have awakened their Kundalini, raised it, and become enlightened without ever having restrained their breath for meditation purposes. There is no "one way only" of achieving Freedom. What is proposed in this book is merely a Kundalini Yoga approach, which albeit extremely powerful, might not be the fastest or best way for some individuals.

In that case, my suggestion is as follows:

Instead of practicing Kriya Supreme Fire, you should do whatever practice makes your mind still. That could be something like a simple mantra meditation, a pranayama, etc[14]. Then, proceed to rest in the post-practice state of being for the rest of the time. Again, that is the most important yet

---

[14] Remember some of the "add-on methods" known to strongly awaken the Kundalini, such as Mula Bandha, Uddiyana Bandha, breath-retention, Root or Crown focus. Since breath-retention is out of the equation, you can always try to incorporate any of the others into your practice, if you wish, before the "just being" state.

overlooked part of any routine, and does not involve any kind of restraint, mudra, bandha, or some special technique.

Don't beat yourself up for not being able to do Kriya Supreme Fire. Things don't happen randomly, and there is a big chance that due to not being able to restrain the breath, you were actually led to a practice that will suit you better in the long run.

Even if you have no health problems and can restrain your breath, you might still prefer to take this approach. It's simple, and it definitely works. There may be fewer fireworks and experiences, but these are not a requirement for enlightenment anyway.

CHAPTER 10

KUNDALINI AWAKENING CONSEQUENCES AND GROUNDING

For some practitioners, the awakening of Kundalini can also bring unwanted consequences. As we've talked about in the prior chapters, there will be many "positives" (that will outweigh any "negatives"), and there may be some less positive symptoms, primarily related to the "fire" (rage, aggressiveness, headaches, etc.).

How many side-effects you experience always depends on your level of ripeness and spiritual maturity. Some Kundalini awakening signs might also be totally unexpected and seemingly unrelated, ranging from extreme empathy to antisocial tendencies; from sensory over-sensitivity to feeling like you don't live in your body at all; from sudden jerking movements to losing all your strength and falling on the ground, yet staying conscious of everything; etc.

To reduce any unwanted side-effects, it is best to let the body slowly get used to the new levels of energy that will be generated. Headaches, irritability, burning sensations or a "heavy head" might be symptoms of too many head-based practices or forcing the breath-retention too much.

We must channel the new powerful energy in the right way, with auspicious thoughts and motivations, always upward toward the highest centers. The energy can either become a source of tremendous instinctive desire/lust/aggressiveness, or it can lead to emptiness/peace/bliss awareness. This depends on where your thoughts and energy are flowing and being stored.

The awakening of the Kundalini energy might be too premature for many people, but I am sure this book will reach the hands of those who are ready for it. When you are ready, God/Life/Spirit/*Satguru* provides. A "higher intelligence" knows exactly what it is doing; it's not up to me. Above all, it depends on your surrenderness and earnestness.

By not rushing, doing some asana-based practices, and following the grounding tips that I will share, your subtle body will gradually become ready to be able to handle the cosmic energy.

Just so you understand how powerful this spiritual practice is, there is a similar practice in Tibetan Buddhism. Before

Buddhist monks are allowed to do this inner-fire practice, they have to go through a series of preliminaries, like practicing loving-kindness meditation for years, and on top of all that, they live in freezing regions. A cold environment reduces the chances of experiencing any side-effects like aggressiveness, rage, fury, sexual impulsiveness, etc. Understand how potent what you have in your hands is, giving it the necessary value and attention.

Due to the tremendous power this practice generates, it will unlock a lot of unconscious pollution you might have accumulated throughout this life (or others), including deep-rooted fears. These can be painful to experience, but on the other hand, there will also be many incredibly blissful experiences to compensate. Remember that Liberation is freeing yourself from ego constraints, not burying more traumas.

If too many side-effects occur, you can try practicing Kriya Supreme Fire standing, rather than sitting. I know this sounds weird, but some people report good results this way. There is a chance that your body will start to shake during the Supreme Fire practice. By practicing standing, the shaking will expand toward the legs instead of just the upper body. When the energy extends to the legs, it gets less concentrated in the head and torso. Besides that, the legs connect you to the ground and can help you release the excess energy through the feet. Because the practice is so intense, it can eject your consciousness into different realms, which if often done, can make you lose contact with this physical world and make you feel depressed every time you "come back." In a few rare cases, some practitioners will want to spend more time in their "inner dimensions" than in here, the physical realm. It's not that there is any issue with that, but if you are here on planet Earth right now, there is a purpose for it.

We should try to generate and accumulate the greatest amount of energy possible without any side-effects. For this to happen, all of the excess energy must be discharged. Having a good "down-flow" capacity will help you reach higher states of consciousness and ecstasy without losing grounding in the world.

In some cases, there might occur something similar to the fight-or-flight response, as the brain thinks you are going to die. Of course, this practice will not kill you, it's actually the opposite—you will feel alive like never before.

As a general rule, if something feels bad, the first thing to do is to reduce the breath-retention time and go very slowly, self-pacing as necessary. If you are doing a practice where you focus on the Crown Chakra, try switching the focal point to the Third-Eye. In some cases, you can even take a break by stopping the practice and resume it a few days later when you're feeling better. Perhaps practicing full Kriya Yoga rather than Kundalini Yoga might be more appropriate. The overall energetic effects are the same, but Kriya is gentler.

Interacting with nature is the best way to get grounded. Walking barefoot in a forest, on a beach, or connecting with animals, trees and plants will help you discharge all of the excess energy. This is a very peaceful, easy and joyful way to get grounded. Swimming in the sea also has a similar effect.

Eating heavier food or in larger quantity in general will also make your system expend extra energy on digestion, which means it will have less energy for spiritual purposes, thus lowering any side-effects you might have.

As it has been mentioned before, doing asanas or physical exercise will help tremendously in regulating the energy. It's also one of the most fun and beneficial grounding exercises you can do, because it will improve your overall health, from muscles to bones to the cardiovascular and pulmonary system, etc. Three good asanas for this purpose are *uttanasana* (standing forward bend), *anuvittasana* (standing backbend) and *paschimottanasana* (seated forward bend with each leg and then both legs at the same time, like in Kriya Yoga's Maha Mudra). If you sleep properly and do 15-20 minutes of asanas per day and/or 30-45 minutes of bodyweight or weightlifting exercises twice a week, you will reduce any side-effects by 90%.

As a *last resort*, here's a controversial grounding tip: relax! Do something you enjoy that you haven't done in a while that is totally "non-spiritual," something that is considered mundane by the spiritual community. Whether they are right or not may be arguable, but one thing is for certain: it will help you expel any excess energy because it makes you descend to a more "human" energy level. In this case, it is not a detour or an excuse to drift away from your purpose of being Free, but rather it's an out-of-the-box way of releasing excess spiritual energy that your system still can't handle, when nothing else has worked[15]. This is usually unnecessary if you follow any of the grounding tips aforementioned whenever unwanted symptoms occur.

Regardless of whether you have any side-effects or not, you should do a careful self-analysis every day, seeing how you feel. In any case, if you can overcome all possible distress, the prize will be huge. Eventually, any side-effects will vanish, and the whole practice will become peaceful and gentle.

---

[15] Please be aware that this does *not* mean you cannot do those "mundane" things that you enjoy whenever you wish. This is being written as a last resort grounding tip, and must not be taken out of context.

Part 3

CHAPTER 11

THE TURNING POINT

When the Kundalini Shakti reaches the Crown Chakra, your consciousness is no longer the individual consciousness you used to know—it has now expanded toward Universal Consciousness. A powerful ecstatic experience catapults the usually limited consciousness toward blissful heights never experienced before. It is like a warm, rich and potent energy has merged with a crystalline, heightened thoughtless awareness.

Once all prana has been absorbed and stabilized in the central channel, and the Kundalini is in the Crown Chakra, the tremendous bliss generated there will cause it to "melt," softly. This "experience" is of a magnitude that no words can do justice to it. It's the beginning of the true *Shaktipat*[16], very

---

[16] The full Shaktipat is when the Kundalini has finally reposed in the Spiritual Heart, which requires a tremendous surrenderness, often equated with "Grace."

different from any *shaktipat* that occurs in initiations where the guru supposedly ignites the Kundalini in the disciple.

For many, this is the turning point where they realize that bliss, happiness, and peace come from within, and not from outside. A sense of non-attachment toward the world and all of its diverse faces will emerge. The real spiritual life begins here.

Some might experience an absolute silent void where you completely forget yourself (who you think you are, your personality), which when encountered multiple times, might feel like an impenetrable wall. At this point, the best is to try to be aware of who is aware of the void. It might be difficult to do it the very first time you experience such "void," but with time, you will have the intuitive "remembrance" to "do" it. This will break the wall.

Although this "union" of the inner fire with empty conscious-ness can bring mystical and cosmic experiences, unforgettable visions, nectarine divine bliss, and so on, you will sooner or later start noticing that those experiences are not happening as often nor lasting as long as you'd like. They don't last forever. If you hold on to any experience, you are allowing yourself to be disappointed. It is their nature to come and go.

Many yogis or spiritual practitioners get stuck at this stage, always wanting more and more experiences, ecstasies and

Kundalini explosions. By now you ought to know that ephemeralness, which is the essence of all those experiences, is not Freedom. We will pass through this stage and keep going, toward *That* which is both beyond the temporary and the permanent, for it is beyond time. It is time to stop ascending, and use the pure state of mind that we've achieved to turn around 180° degrees and demolish everything that is not us. Contrasting with the current self-help/ pseudo-spiritual trend, you should know this truth:

Genuine spirituality is not about improving our personality (self-development). It is about destroying the illusion we have of ourselves.

THE "I-EGO" IS THE TROUBLE

You came here empty-handed, and you will leave empty-handed. Some advanced practitioners might think they are not attached to anything. Worldly pleasures do not interest them the least. Yet they are still attached—attached to their "I." Many have created a spiritual ego, a subtle and astute "I."

We spend our lives attached to material things, substances, people, thought patterns, emotions, our history, our personality, etc. Spiritual traditions say that we must purify and clean away all that dirt, and although that is useful at the beginning to make the mind more mature, you must realize that it is just like cutting the branch off of a tree. It will grow up again, in a different or similar manner. What's the point? We must remove the tree by its root, and then the problem will be solved. The root is "I." Only after "I" can "otherness" appear. Only with an "I" can a "you" appear. Only with an "I" can separateness appear to exist. Let this intuitive knowledge arise in your mind, not in thoughts, but in thoughtless *knowingness.*

Our personal "I" creates all the differences. Every true spiritual path, from all worldly traditions, is pointing at something beyond the mind, beyond our little concept we have of who we think we are.

No more should you cling to the transient comfort of this "I," for the immutable certainty of an impersonal divine profundity must now be genuinely recognized.

Once we accept this invitation to be one, rather than two, we will advance through the puzzles of human life in this world without fear and sorrow.

Joy and love are our true One Home.

CHAPTER 12

THE SECRET KUNDALINI THRONE

There is a little-known subtle passage from the Sahasrara Chakra to the Spiritual Heart or Causal Center, which is called *Atma Nadi* or *Amrita Nadi*. After the culmination in the thousand-petaled lotus, the Kundalini descends via this channel into the "Cave of the Heart," also known as the "void of nothingness," where it will repose and dissolve completely. During this descent, some practitioners might experience "flashes" or "extremely subtle vibrations" due to the ecstatic aliveness and conscious awakening of the Amrita Nadi, which is not the same as perceiving the radiant luminosity of the Sushumna Nadi. None of these effects are a requirement, though, and most of the time they will not happen.

The body is insentient, it has no "I" or self-consciousness, while Consciousness is eternal and self-luminous. The "I-ego" is a link between both, between spirit and matter, like a knot (granthi). If we investigate the essence of this "knot of ignorance," we discover that it is only forgetfulness of who we are, which in turn causes us to identify with the body. This ignorance arouses desires for external things to fill our assumed lack of completeness, and thus brings about action to obtain those very things that we believe will fulfill us. Of course, as we already know by now, none of those things will permanently satisfy us. It is this discernment that brings some beings to the spiritual path with the purpose of awakening the Kundalini and being enlightened.

Once we are successful and the Kundalini reaches the Crown Chakra, seeking its source or the source of "I" will take it directly to the Spiritual Heart. There, the "knot of ignorance" is cut, and the I-ego dissolves completely.

If it never reemerges again, that is true enlightenment. That individuality/jiva recognizes itself to be the Absolute/God/Consciousness and no ego-self identification ever happens again. Yet we could say that a "transcendental-I" emerges from the Spiritual Heart, going up through the Amrita Nadi until the Crown Chakra, completely enlightened and aware of its true nature as pure limitless non-dual Consciousness. From Sahasrara, the light of consciousness passes again through the nerves to all parts of the body and thus experiences the world again.

There's a big difference though: no longer will this "I" see everything as separate from itself, but the whole Universe will be its body. The whirl of samsara doesn't bind it anymore. The life-force current in the nerves will be like a phantom rope—it won't bind the "I" ever again, for the "I" is now pure and transcendental.

What once was blinding darkness now gives rise to the sprout of pure and supreme Knowledge.

ENTERING INTO THE SPIRITUAL HEART

Physical heart? Slightly to the left of one's sternum, or breastbone. It's a physical organ.

Energetic heart? Located in the central channel of the spine, in the heart/dorsal region; it is called Anahata and just like the other chakras, it can be seen with the inner vision as a vortex of energy.

Spiritual Heart? Not well-known.

When the Kundalini descends, we recognize the existence of this extremely subtle "space" which can be intuitively felt two digits to the right of the center of the chest. Many yogis consider this "space" to be above the Crown Chakra, but on a closer investigation, one can "see" that the 8th and higher chakras are "subtler versions" of the original seven chakras. On the contrary, the Spiritual Heart is different from all the chakras as it is not an energetic plexus. It can be said to be the void of nothingness, a vast endless space that contains the whole universe and all dimensions, including all chakras, no matter how subtle they are. This intuitive and inner "apperception" is not a normal subject-object perceiving, but more like a non-phenomenal *knowingness*, which defies logic and common language.

The great sage Ramana Maharshi sometimes made mention of the Spiritual Heart, but besides him, one or two other recent Gurus, and some rare ancient texts, we seldom find any information about it in the yogic or spiritual literature. It was usually omitted from written works because this teaching was reserved only for the "high initiates," in a direct Guru-to-disciple transmission.

Yet if we pay attention to certain passages, we can find some subtle mentions. For example, let's take a look at a brief section of Paramahansa Yogananda's Samadhi description from *Autobiography of a Yogi* (1946):

> "I cognized the center of the empyrean as a *point of intuitive perception in my heart*."

Here's a quote from the *Maitrayaniya Upanishad*:

"The shrine which consists of the ether [space] in the heart, the blissful, the highest retreat [treasure], that is our own, that is our goal, and that is the heat and brightness of the fire and the Sun"

Although the whole of creation is nothing but Consciousness, the original *bindu* (point) from where it all emerged can be said to be the Spiritual Heart, or the "space of the Heart" as it's called in the Upanishads. It is from here that the universe emerges and to where it is withdrawn. Every time the "I" comes to this Heart space unconsciously, it seems to be ignorance (unconscious states). But by resting in Consciousness/Beingness, the practitioner discovers that this space is no longer the dark unconscious state that it was once thought to be, but instead reflects the pure light of Self, of Consciousness. When this happens, the "I" that once blindly believed "I am this body-mind," now realizes its true nature, and undoubtedly *knows* beyond any concept of "knowing," beyond thought, "I am pure Consciousness." The mind, now identified with that "light," is a perfect stainless mirror that reflects *Oneness* (non-duality) in this illusive *manyness* (duality). Self-Knowledge (*Atma-jnana*) is now its root, rather than the dark ignorance of separation.

Nevertheless, these explanations are merely to give you a "sense" of comprehension and insight, because although they are correct, on a deeper level we have to go further and realize that the "Spiritual Heart" is not a "place" or even a "space," but rather the underlying primal boundless pure Consciousness that we really are.

This means that no spiritual practice (movement of the mind) will help you enter into the Spiritual Heart. Only Being can do so. Being (stillness) is not a spiritual practice because it's the opposite of doing (movement). For it to happen, the practitioner needs to have an earnest desire for Self-Realization and a complete surrender. After reaching the Crown, simply stay as the witness Consciousness, without any other adjunct, and you will arrive in the Spiritual Heart. When properly done, it will throw the whole "I" into a consuming blissful fire, taking hold of the life-force and entering into the Spiritual Heart, withdrawing the entire mind from the hypnotic world of names and forms into the non-dual space-like Consciousness.

Many practitioners make the mistake of trying to concentrate on some space two digits to the right of one's chest. That's not correct. Only by being, by staying as "I am" (the Kriya Yoga's Parvastha) will you "enter" into the Spiritual Heart. I know I'm repeating, but it's essential. Do not forget it.

Now, can the Spiritual Heart be experienced?

The "experience of nothingness" from deep dreamless sleep and general unconscious states could be considered an experience of the Spiritual Heart, untranslatable to the mind, thus being called "nothingness." Yet we call it nothingness only because we're so used to the feeling of "I," which when not present makes us only aware of its absence, like removing a ring that you've worn for so long makes you only notice that it's not there rather than noticing the "ring-less" finger itself.

The Spiritual Heart might sound like a complicated teaching, but hopefully the following example will clear all doubts:

Let's suppose a mirror is lying on the grass in an open space, reflecting the sunlight. This reflection passes through a tiny hole in the wall of a windowless pitch-black house, illuminating it, and allowing whoever lives in that house to see. The ego-mind is this ray of reflected light, enabling perceiving in what would otherwise be just a dark "house."

If we investigate from where the light that illuminates the house is coming from, we will find the hole. Upon looking through that tiny hole, we will actually see the Sun. It will look like the Sun is located somewhere in the grass, outside of the house. We can point out that the Sun is in the grass, in an exact place. But if we investigate even further and leave the house following the ray of light, how surprised we will be when we find out that it's not the Sun! It is a mirror reflecting the Sun! The Spiritual Heart is that mirror. That is where the

I-ego/mind (reflected sunlight) comes from. But that's not really the Sun! When we get to the mirror, the reflected ray of light is no more. Due to our habitual feeling of "I," we will conclude that there's "nothingness," since there is no more "I" (reflection) anywhere. This is the "experience of nothingness," and it is what happens unconsciously during deep sleep. One thing is different, though. We did not come to the mirror unconsciously, and so we look up to the sky. Lo and behold, there is the Sun! The Sun is pure formless Consciousness, not bound to any place, but all-pervading.

Journeying from our limited ego toward the Spiritual Heart is the greatest journey a human can undertake. When the "I" is liberated from the bodily tangle and melted in the ocean of Consciousness, there will be the realization of the Truth that *everything* is Consciousness, the Self. The idea of being a separate entity has been destroyed. The natural state of blissful, ever-present peace and Oneness, usually called *Turiya*[17], prevails.

---

[17] Turiya means the "Fourth State," the substratum of the three states of waking, dreaming and sleeping.

CHAPTER 13

COSMIC KUNDALINI

Your true Self is God, unmanifested, but because of your attachments, you again come back into ego-body identification. You must now give up such identification, and let the body's activities continue while not identifying with them. This loss of "doership" can be accomplished only by diving our present consciousness into the depths of unconsciousness, with the Kundalini itself, which like a bright comet journeying through dark space, awakens us into our cosmic home. This is such a blessing that we should enjoy our Self-perceived universal greatness, which is completely innocent, emanating boundless love toward every sentient and insentient form. Yet there will come a time when in the midst of being *Ishvara* (God manifested), a subtle inquiry arises in the very core of our expansive beingness: a "perceiving" is still happening. Who is the perceiver?

What are you supposed to "do" in such a situation? You look back to who is perceiving or witnessing that and repose in that background, that blissful Self-Awareness state. This bliss of Being, where nothing is perceived because our consciousness is reposing as bliss itself, being absorbed into the Spiritual Heart, dissolves everything we are not until what is left is the indescribable Absolute, *Parabrahman*. That's where the Kundalini's cosmic journey will take us.

Kundalini is not different from Consciousness because everything is Consciousness. However, Kundalini is not static consciousness but dynamic consciousness, the purest vibration. In its pristine form, Kundalini can be equated with the "transcendental I," Universal Mind, Universal Consciousness or as some call it, the adjunctless "I am."

Pure Consciousness (Shiva) is immutable, unmovable, non-dual. There is no "I" there. It is beyond being personal or impersonal, and there's no point trying to give more attributes and labels to That which nothing can define. When it manifests as this magnificent cosmos, it does so as energy, as the Cosmic Kundalini. Cosmic Kundalini is Shakti, whose nature is pure bliss (ananda).

In the beginning, the first manifestation of pure Consciousness is "I am." This "I am" goes even further into duality and diversity, manifesting as all the sentient beings, for example.

When the Cosmic Kundalini comes up from the Spiritual Heart to the brain region, and then spreads toward the whole nervous system as prana, it is no longer the impersonal "I am." It gets transmuted into a "limited-consciousness" which is called "ego-mind," the personal "I am this body."

When we gather all this prana back into the central channel, up to the brain region and Crown, and then to the Spiritual Heart, we go beyond all duality. If it reaches Sahasrara only, the cosmic Samadhi experienced will not be enough for Self-Realization (*Sahaja Samadhi*, the natural and effortless non-dual state of enlightenment).

The Crown Chakra is like the Moon. It reflects the light of the Spiritual Heart, which is the Sun.

As is said in *Kriya Yoga Exposed*, if you had to point to "I," where would you point? Definitely not to the head. It's always to the Heart region. There is where the "I" emerges and where it ends.

Despite the seeming duality between the Shiva and Shakti, they are actually one and the same. We use different terms to explain Consciousness and Energy so that the human mind has a better "grasp" of what lies beyond. It is no wonder that the mind (hence separateness) likes to separate things in order to better understand them, always trying to dissect the Oneness. With the creation of the manifest world, Shiva (pure Consciousness) stays transcendental and beyond space-time, while Shakti (energy) remains inherent to duality, giving life to everything. Shakti is what manifests as Life and universal beauty. Yet it is inseparable from pure Consciousness just like the burning power is inseparable from fire.

When Consciousness is conscious of existing, of purely Being, it is blissful. Since Consciousness can never not be conscious of Being—unless it covers itself with an illusory veil—it is ever blissful. Being-Consciousness-Bliss (Sat-Chit-Ananda), a term often used to denote our true nature, is Shiva-Shakti. Being-Consciousness (Sat-Chit) is Shiva while Bliss (Ananda) is Shakti. They are indivisible!

CHAPTER 14

SPIRITUALITY IS NOT SUBTLE ENTERTAINMENT

Experiences can change lives. Besides being the most powerful teaching method, a powerful experience can switch your life goal from something mundane and superficial to the most auspicious objective of human life. Having a glimpse of something deeper than this earthly existence has not only changed the lives of some whose goal was to become the most successful or richest person in the world, but also of those who were "hardcore skeptics." Most "spirituality" is indeed made of experiences, and many seekers just want to satisfy their curiosity. That's all fine, but if you desire to go further into the mystery of existence, there will come a time where you have to go beyond all experiences and techniques.

If you wanted to go from Sidney to New York City, you would first catch a taxi to take you to the airport. Upon arriving, you would leave the taxi and board the airplane. You would not bring the taxi with you. It will have served its purpose but then it must be discarded, or you'll never catch the airplane. In the same way, there comes a time when we leave all experiences and techniques behind so that we can catch the airplane of Beingness. I know this is tough, but I have no illusions that people will recognize such a truth, let alone follow it. This direction is for those practitioners whose discernment has been awakened to a *high degree*.

If the benefits of meditation occurred only when we practiced the techniques or had experiences, they would be temporary and have little value, just like everything in the world. Techniques and experiences are merely the means to an end (Self-Realization). We want to bring ever-present love, peace, happiness, wisdom, and unity into our lives, and eventually dissolve in them, rather than getting lost in experience after experience.

Continually chasing experiences and practicing spiritual techniques for all your life will only reinforce duality and the belief that you are a practitioner, a meditator, or even a body. All bodies are illusions, from the gross to the subtle and even to the causal. They are just maps or ideas that assist the seeker in understanding different types of experiences or supposed signposts.

For example, the experience of being space, or being "everywhere and everything," is a subtle body experience. It is the "I am" at its finest level. The "experience of nothingness" is a causal body experience which everyone experiences in deep sleep.

You can try to analyze and understand all those experiences; that is perfectly natural. Just don't lose yourself in trying to find a logical answer for everything. It leads nowhere.

Every spiritual tradition explains things differently, often with a religious/devotional tone, which pushes many people away. They all do it, from the esoteric teachings of something like *Kabbalah* to Buddhism to Hinduism, etc. These days, that doesn't seem the best way to go, and most people run away from anything that resembles a religious overtone. However, the word "religion" originally meant "Re-Connect," which is synonymous with "reconnect with your true nature, which you now seem to have forgotten." With that being said, due to thousands of years of misuse, the original meaning has been forgotten, and it now implies "blindly believe in something someone told you."

That leads many to try to understand these experiences scientifically. Impressed by the clever inventiveness and findings of the scientists, they base their understanding on scientific evidence and offer it as an interpretation.

That can work up to a point using quantum physics, modern

neuroscience, and cutting-edge psychology, but it's also limited when it reaches a certain depth. The exploration of consciousness is a subject-based investigation, not object-based. Moreover, the imperishable and infinite Consciousness will always shine forth unimpeded by the scope of empirical evidence.

The truth is that Self-Realization cannot be adequately explained in such a way. More often than not, one sees the futility of trying to explain the mystery of Consciousness through scientific methods. It's like being in a dream where the dream characters are trying to "solve" or "dissect" the nature of the dream or Consciousness with "dream-tools," "dream-senses," and "dream-laws." It will never work unless they are willing to question the dreamer, the observer of the dream rather than the dream itself! The ways often used to find out and explain the Truth are actually part of the illusion. How can they ever show or really decipher the Truth?

Max Planck, the father of quantum physics and winner of the Nobel Prize in Physics in 1918, echoes this perfectly:

> "Science cannot solve the ultimate mystery of nature. And that is because, in the last analysis, we ourselves are a part of the mystery that we are trying to solve."
>
> - WHERE IS SCIENCE GOING? (1932)

Science cannot give us all of the ultimate answers because it's bounded by its own rules that everything must be studied objectively; but you can, by becoming aware of all the unconscious parts of your current limited existence as this body-mind, realizing they are not who you truly are, and seeking the source of the experiencing subject, "I."

There is no doubt that all experiences and concentration-induced Samadhis might help you in this quest for Self-discovery, diminishing the limited idea you have of yourself—but it is the willingness to dissolve in the unified presence of Being that finally does it.

CHAPTER 15

THE BACKGROUND PRESENCE OF BEING

For the full Kundalini effect, there must be the merging of energy practices with consciousness/witness practices. This is merging Bliss with Emptiness or Energy with Consciousness, depending on which terms you prefer.

Energetic practices on their own will not lead you all the way to enlightenment. True wisdom and discernment must be cultivated and awakened by the Self-Awareness state of just being. This has been mentioned throughout the book, and the reason why is that it's such a difficult teaching to imprint that usually the practitioner needs to read or hear it from multiple angles in multiple different contexts to allow it to sink in. This state not only helps to clear most of our attachments, subtle tendencies, and desires, but is also essential in bringing the Kundalini to its final reposing place. The Buddha said these two were the cornerstones of enlightenment, and called them *Samatha*, which is one-pointed meditation that culminates in effortless, joyful attention, and *Vipassana*, which is self-introspection through abiding in awareness and having insight into the nature of reality[18], which are terms very poorly understood these days. One-pointed meditation elevates the mind to a tranquil state, from which arises equanimity—the perfect base for resting in the background witness or Self-Awareness state. Abiding and melting in that background produces a non-intellectual direct realization of our true nature. Does this sound familiar? Yes, it is the same "strategy" we use in Kriya Yoga. Different traditions transmit the Truth in various ways, but with a sharp discernment one can see that they are all talking about the same thing! *A rose is still a rose no matter what name we wish to give it.*

Bliss-Emptiness can be "experienced" through either the suspension of breath or by the melting of thought. This is not an unconscious empty mind or anything like that, but rather an intense Self-Awareness empty of any objective knowledge. What it "knows" is itself, which is pure Being-Bliss.

Letting go of all demands, of all wants, of all doings, even if they are spiritual in nature or noble in cause, there arises the *knowingness* of what is already here, of what is already

---

[18] Not to be confused with the "Vipassana movement" of observing body sensations.

ever-present and ever-available. This presence of Being might seem very subtle at first, underlying the whole experience of life, yet it is cosmic and mighty. It is in this background of Consciousness or Presence-state that you have to abide.

Vigilance and alertness play a big role, at least in the beginning, preventing you from re-identifying with the mind. When thoughts start appearing and you feel you are about to lose this state, a strategy to prevent it from ending is inquiring "Who is perceiving these thoughts?" This will make the attention go back to itself, the subject, and thoughts will dissolve. Of course, this will need dedication and perseverance. However, since you've been doing the Kriya Supreme Fire technique, your awareness will be blasted into this post-practice state without notice. Once you get used to dwelling there consciously, it will be much harder for it to "end."

The truth is that it never ends. It is our habitual pattern of ego-identification that seems to return and superimpose itself on the space-like Consciousness. In this state, we have no desires, no needs, and no requirements. We are at peace.

Gently but powerfully, we will recognize the love and happiness of Being, and we will want nothing else. The more we abide in it, the more the Kundalini is brought into the seat of the Heart. Our personality and physiology go through immense changes, becoming more *sattvic* (pure) in nature, allowing themselves to be more and more absorbed by the peaceful presence.

The more you simply ARE, the more depth and beauty you will have as a human being. Sometimes your heart will feel "heavy," but in a good way, like it's full of a warm love and joy that are so immense that it can't contain. It feels like it's about to explode in tears of tenderness.

When you start experiencing moments of "I-less awareness," you will not recognize that you were in a "no-mind" state. Only afterward, when these gaps become bigger and bigger will you certainly know what it is to BE.

That will not happen during "sitting practices" only, but will actually expand and permeate your whole life with a beauty that cannot be named, something indescribable, a divine outpouring of a love that knows no limits.

Through being present, thought becomes absorbed in a void, which then gives place to bliss, dissolving the false sense of objectivity and duality. Ultimately, the ego disappears, and only pure non-dual Consciousness remains. Finding out for yourself how this nameless aroma of the Absolute will take you all the way to its Self-recognition is a marvelous discovery.

CHAPTER 16

THE DISSOLUTION OF KUNDALINI

The goal of Yoga is the complete suppression of the waves in the ocean of the mind. When the waves of thoughts stop, there is immense bliss. It is the restless mind that does not allow us to be joyful all the time.

When the Kundalini dissolves into the Spiritual Heart, life will be an ocean of peace and happiness. This means that the sense of "I" *as we know it*, which is constantly being reinforced in the individual, is no longer operating. Without "I," there is no selfishness, no egotism. This is the condition from which all human beings should operate. When there is no ego self, the Supreme Self stands revealed. That's the final purpose of the Kundalini.

For those who live through the mind only, there is duality, the triad of the seer, seeing, and seen. Their center of consciousness is in the brain-area. For those who live from the

Spiritual Heart, whose center is everywhere and circumference nowhere, no such duality exists. It's one all-encompassing Unity. Unlike the I-ego, which is limited to the body-mind, there are no limits to one's being.

While previously the "I" was living from the assumption of being the finite, manifested and mortal self, the "transcendental-I" is living from the *knowingness* that is the unmanifested, infinite and deathless Self.

Enlightenment, although it might seem like a fancy word, is just liberation from the slavery imposed by the ego! Thoughts will no longer control you, and you will live in peace and joy unattached to anything whatsoever. If you need to "think" about something, like booking an airplane ticket, you will use the mind. But it will not force you to overthink and become lost in thought or to live in your head and in your memories. You will be free from all that. You will naturally be present, happy and free.

The fleeting joy is no more, for it is ever-present, all-flowing, everywhere, nowhere and beyond. This is your natural state. Supreme Freedom, Self-Awareness and Supreme Bliss are synonymous.

You used to be afraid to cross the river to the other side, where happiness and Freedom reside. You once saw a sea snake, and subsequently every time you tried to cross the river, you got scared and backed off. Now a voice comes from the other side and says, "It's only a piece of wood. It looks like a sea snake but isn't." You are shocked. Now you know that the sea snake, which is the idea "I am imprisoned," has never been true. It was a hoax all along.

Whenever there is duality, multiplicity, it is an illusory dream. It is not real.

Take the waves, for example: they are always moving, washing up against the shore. That's what they do. They live with the idea of separateness, never finding their eternal wholeness.

One day a group of waves decided to search for the ocean. They searched everywhere, but could never find it. "It seems like there is no ocean!" said the smartest wave who was the chief investigator of the quest, "If there were, we would've found it by now. Since we haven't seen it with our own eyes, we can only reason that there is no such thing as the ocean."

One of the waves was not in conformity with the result of their search, so it decided to investigate on its own. Fearlessly, it decided to dive deep within. What that wave found was mesmerizing: the vast ocean! There were no waves, only the one undivided ocean. You are that wave!

We are all coming back to our common source. We are "coming back" to the Self-recognition of our true Being. It is inevitable. Whenever you aspire for true Freedom, the whole

Universe has your back. It is time you say no to the ego and discover your true nature. I know you will succeed. When every one of us loses the sense of separateness, real equality and peace will reign on Earth. The planet Earth can then be a single family.

CHAPTER 17

THE DIVINE AND THE ORDINARY

All blisses, ecstasies, mystical visions and encounters, all experiences—they happened. Now—they're gone. A simple, blissful life takes over. In spite of whatever happens outside, unbroken peace is the constant. "Bliss" is not even the proper word to use, for the natural state is blissful beyond the need of being blissful. The mind can never figure that out. It's a completeness beyond being the contrary of limitedness.

At the beginning of our journey, we had to realize what we are not. We peeled off the onion until only the core remained. The core is pure Consciousness. Now, we recognize that everything we had to ditch—is also us. But not in the same way as we once considered. The mind, the Universe, the Earth, the body, nature, emotions, life, death… they are the fragrance of the orchid of Being. They are not apart from us; they are the vehicle with which Consciousness can express its infinite love for itself. Duality is how Consciousness tastes experience.

There is no separation between inside and outside, "divine" and "human."

The ordinary is divine.

The divine is ordinary.

The ordinary becomes extraordinary.

The extraordinary is ordinary.

There is no differentiation between the external and the internal.

There is no difference between God and the devotee, Shiva and Shakti, Brahman and Maya.

Duality is non-duality.

We are the whole Universe. And we are nothing. May you realize that both are the same.

We will never truly live while still bound by the chains of desire and selfishness, for they make us carry the burden of incompleteness, always binding us to this empty dream.

Enlightenment is not reserved for the very few. Nobody is the chosen one. Very few become enlightened because very few *really* want it above everything else.

Are you doing something every day that takes you closer to the recognition of your true Self?

Are you aware of your daily reactions, thoughts, and behaviors? Are they contributing to your Self-Realization?

Are you catching your ego's constant defense mechanisms? Do you notice how it subtly tricks you into wasting time and energy on things that will only lead you to the temporary?

Do you act as if no other living creature is better or worse than you?

Are you really interested in achieving Liberation? Are you willing to do what it takes?

Are you willing to let go of your history, your achievements, your dream-goals and your personality?

If you are really interested in finding God, the Truth, your true Self, then these are the kind of questions you should be asking.

Zombieing through the senses, one day a hand will reach out to you and mirror your real Being, reminding you who you are so that you can recover your never-lost eternity. You are looking in the mirror now. Let your Heart show you the beauty of who you are, miraculously unfolding the perennial cosmic dance of the Infinite.

Resting in the Self, as the Self, worldly activities are spontaneously occurring while you witness them with utmost joy. To "live" in non-duality even while duality seemingly unrolls, is the ultimate *roar of Love* of the beatific existence of Consciousness.

We are the single dweller amid the all-pervading boundless sanctuary of existence.

CHAPTER 18

"WHAT I REALLY WANT"

Do you remember the very first chapter of this book?

You, reader, think about what you really want. Think deeply.

Yes, exactly, "that" which you want.

Now, near the end of this book, you have probably realized that what you want is to be "enlightened," "Self-realized," or even "liberated," which are all synonymous with "perfectly fulfilled," "totally happy," and "eternally in peace."

Do you know what? Those are just thoughts and ideas that you have about what those concepts are. It is that very *person* who wants to be "enlightened" that prevents you from achieving that goal—being enlightened.

Your ideas of what "enlightenment," "Self-realization" or "Freedom" are, are *not* what That is. What That is, is beyond any concepts or ideas you might have.

That is what I've been trying to "show" you in all of my books. No, not the words themselves but the glimpse of the *inexplicableness* that you *feel* deep inside when reading them. You know it because you already are it! How can't you?

It's time to reclaim what you've never lost.

Do not look for something else; look for nothing besides yourself, for "What You Really Want" is yourself. You are That which you are looking for. Even if you don't know it yet, one day you will. Everyone will. And everyone will know that they never knew anything else besides That that they don't seem to know now. How wonderful That Is!

AUTHOR'S MESSAGE

Don't be afraid of awakening the Kundalini. I guarantee you that by reading this book, your degree of mind purity will increase tenfold. The mind will attune itself to the frequency of the energy behind these words, which is pure, non-dogmatic, and with genuine intentions. Use it as a bridge to gain motivation, inspiration, awaken discernment and go even deeper in your beingness.

Don't forget to commit to your spiritual practice. If you have any doubts, shoot me an email and I will do my best to help you. Don't live your whole life afraid of not being ready. You are ready.

I assure you that you already have all you need inside you, not just to awaken the Kundalini, but to achieve liberation *in this lifetime*. Ultimately, two words come up again and again: earnestness and surrenderness.

These are the two key ingredients you need. They have brought you here.

The teachings in this series are the best that I've ever received, both internally and externally, from the most varied sources, without any dogmatic imprint, and in a condensed and direct format. None of the teachings shared in these books belong to me—they are universal.

I have never written anything until recently. Suddenly, an immense urge to write emerged, and countless words have manifested from the depths of my consciousness. With my background in Kriya and Kundalini Yoga, I decided to first expose the dogmatic yogic teachings of today's world in *Kriya Yoga Exposed*, not with the purpose of degrading anyone, but to help others awaken a higher inner discernment that will help them realize that most teachings, although perhaps genuine in intention, lack "directness" and "absolute truthfulness" to say the least. Then, with a higher understanding and an open-mind, sincere seekers can finally dive into nonduality, burning through all misconceptions, labels, desires, tendencies, and egotism, realizing their true Self.

The natural flow of life tells me that these words are helping people all over the world, and that I should continue doing so. I honestly don't know for how long this body-mind will be writing, but for now, the fountain of wisdom and love just keeps manifesting into words. May you find usefulness in them as a valuable guidepost back Home. I always try to write in simple, uncomplicated English, without too much fanciness. You may dislike or disagree with what is written, but know that I still have your back. Even those who hate these books or have said negative things about them, it is fine. I still love you and hope you find teachings that better suit your predispositions.

Anyhow, if you have any questions or doubts, you can email me at ***Santata@RealYoga.info*** and I will gladly help you. You can also subscribe at ***www.RealYoga.info*** and download a free ebook called *Uncovering the Real*. You'll also be the first to know about new books, articles, etc. I usually send all that information through the newsletter once or twice a month. I never send anything that is not related to the Truth. If you have subscribed but have not received the confirmation email, or you haven't been receiving the newsletter, perhaps check the junk/spam folder and move them to the inbox or add my email to the contact list.

Since many people have asked about me, all I will say is that I'm neither a "householder," nor a "monk." I live a simple life totally dedicated and surrendered to the Truth. Authentic spiritual teachings are for going beyond the limited personhood into Godhood, which means the "person" is not really worth talking about. As long as we relate to each other as persons, we will not go far.

Many people think they know me, that I am person X or monk Y. All I can say is: I am none of those. I am no one. None of my teachings come from the body-mind, but from something far beyond, something that is ineffable, but not distant. *That which IS* is also available to you here and now. It is You!

I hope I have inspired you to take the necessary steps in your journey so that you can find the joy and peace you've been looking for, and possibly, who knows, realize the boundless Absolute you've always been.

If you enjoyed reading this book and it helped you under-stand the mystery of Kundalini in a deeper way, guiding you into your own being, **please show your support by leaving a *Review on the Amazon page*.**

It really makes a difference.
It helps spreading the true teachings to those who are genuinely seeking them.

Thank you.

Read also, by the same author of *Kundalini Exposed*:

— KRIYA YOGA EXPOSED

The Truth About Current Kriya Yoga Gurus & Organizations. Contains the Explanation of a Special Kriya Technique Never Revealed Before.

— THE SECRET POWER OF KRIYA YOGA

Revealing the Fastest Path to Enlightenment. How Fusing Bhakti & Jnana Yoga into Kriya will Unleash the most Powerful Yoga Ever.

— THE YOGA OF CONSCIOUSNESS

25 Direct Practices to Enlightenment.
Revealing the Missing Key to Self-Realization. Beyond Kundalini, Kriya Yoga & all Spirituality into Awakening Non-Duality.

— TURIYA: THE GOD STATE

Unravel the ancient mystery of Turiya—The God State. The book that demystifies and uncovers the true state of Enlightened beings.

— SAMADHI: THE FORGOTTEN EDEN

Unveiling the ancient art of how yogis and mystics had the keys to an unlimited reservoir of wisdom and power. This book brings the timeless and forgotten wisdom of Samadhi into modern-day practicality.

— THE YOGIC DHARMA

Revealing the underlying essence of the Yamas and Niyamas.
A profound, unconventional, and inspiring exposition on the spirit of the Yogic Dharma principles.

Available @ Amazon as Kindle & Paperback.

GLOSSARY

Agni - The "fire god," but it actually means the inner fire.

Akashic Records - Said to be a compendium of all universal events, thoughts, words, emotions, and intent from the past, present, and future.

Amrita Nadi / Atma Nadi - Final extension of Sushumna Nadi, goes from the brain-area to 2-digits to the right of the center of one's chest.

Atma-Jnana - Self-Knowledge; "Knowing" oneself's true nature.

Bandhas - Bandhas are like valves, locks concerning the energetic system of the body.

Bhajans - Devotional songs.

Bija Mantra - Seed mantras.

Bindu - Dot, point, which is considered to be where Creation first emanated from.

Brahman - The Ultimate Reality, the Absolute. Some call it **Parabrahman**, which means Highest Brahman or Brahman without form or qualities.

Brahmacharya - usually thought to me celibacy, yet according to the definition of Ramana Maharshi, it means "living in *Brahman.*"

Chakra - Wheel/plexus, a psychic-energy center.

Ida Nadi - The left subtle channel.

Ishta-Devata - Personal God; the form one attributes to the formless Consciousness.

Ishvara - God manifested; the "ruler of the Universe" (the meaning varies according to each tradition).

Jiva - Individual self.

Kabbalah - Esoteric spiritual discipline originated in Judaism.

Kumbhaka - breath-retention.

Mahabharata - One of India's two great epics, describing the saga of the Pandavas and the Kauravas.

Mantra - Sacred syllable or word or set of words.

Mudra - "Seal." A hand or whole-body gesture performed for the flow of subtle energies.

Mukti, Liberation, Nirvana, Salvation, Enlightenment & Self-Realization are all synonymous.

Parvastha – The "After-Kriya" blissful Self-Awareness state.

Pingala Nadi - The right subtle channel.

Pranayama - Life-force restraint/control technique.

Sadhana - Spiritual Practice.

Samadhi - Absorption, higher state of consciousness.

Satguru - the true Guru; the inner Guru; God within.

Satsang - Association with being, or, alternatively, being in the presence of a Self-Realized Master.

Shambhavi Mudra - A mudra in which the ocular bulbs and the eyebrows are upturned as much as possible (Crown variation).

Shakti - Personification of Kundalini, the life-force principle that gives life to the Universe.

Shaktipat - An energetic transmission given by the Guru to the disciple; the descent of "divine grace."

Shiva - Personification of the Absolute Consciousness. For some, he is the Hindu God who is the destroyer of the Universe.

Sushumna Nadi - The subtle channel through which the life-force flows, located in the middle of the spine.

Turiya - The fourth state (Self-Realization state).

Ujjayi Breathing - Ocean breathing. It is done by narrowing the throat passage, creating an "ocean" or "rushing" sound by the passage of air, lengthening the inhalation and exhalation. This breathing must be done with the diaphragm, and with "pressure."

Upanishads - The concluding portions of the Vedas.

Vasanas / Samskaras - Latent tendencies stored in the causal body, responsible for reincarnation.

Printed in Great Britain
by Amazon